Songs of Hildegard von Bingen for Harp

arranged by
Monica Schley

Online Audio

To access the online audio go to:
WWW.MELBAY.COM/31151MEB

Cover illustration by Stephen Schildbach

MEL BAY

WWW.MELBAY.COM

Contents

Preface

Hildegard von Bingen (1098-1179) was born in Germany during the Middle Ages, at a time when education and literacy were controlled by the Catholic Church. The tenth child in her family, Hildegard was "given" as a tithing to the church, not an uncommon practice of the time. When she was 14, she was sent to live a life of religious devotion in Disibodenberg. At the convent there, she prayed, wrote, and only had access to the outside world through the view of a single window.

When her main caretaker, Jutta, died in 1136, Hildegard was appointed prioress of the abbey. It was during that time that she began writing music. Despite her claim of lacking formal training in either the Latin language or music, Hildegard produced songs that were equal to those written by the most admired men of the Middle Ages. A woman of letters, she often communicated directly with clergy of the church, including Pope Eugene III, who encouraged her to continue with her writing. She went on to write several books about religion, art, politics, philosophy, science, medicine, and herbs.

Hildegard had visions that she called "reflections of the living light," and she painted what she saw. She had many visitors at the abbey who claimed that she was able to heal them though touch and with her knowledge of herbal medicine. In time, she had so many visitors, that a larger venue was needed. The church relocated her to an abbey of her own, in Bingen, where she was able to attend to more people. Thus, she became known as, Hildegard from Bingen. She died there at the age of 81.

Monica Schley

About This Book

I devised this book with several concepts in mind. First, to honor the work, inspiration, and format of the original compositions by Hildegard von Bingen. At her time, music was largely written monophonically, or single note voicing. Harmonies were either non-existent, or commonly heard as intervals of 4ths or 5ths. Therefore, the beginnings of all these songs have this in mind.

Another element of these songs recognizes their inherent therapeutic nature. Keeping in line with that, I know that these songs work best in their simplest forms. Often therapeutic harpists who play at the bedside for someone unwell will have a small harp, or a folk harp. I wanted to make this music accessible for as many people as possible, so that if the goal was to play for people with physical, mental, or sleep ailments, the therapeutic harpist could do that with the harp size available to them.

Some songs spoke to me in a way that asked for more complexities. I wrote a second arrangement for those pieces. You will see this with five songs: "O Rubor Sanguinis;" "Deus Anim Rorem;" "Deus Enim;" "Under Quocumque;" and "O Cruror Sanguinis." In those second arrangements, you might see low bass notes (for the large harp), sophisticated chords that one didn't hear in the Middle Ages, or space for improvisation and looping of chord progressions. Players should note that "De Patria" can be played in an open meter, rather than strict time.

Monica Schley

Aer Enim

Hildegard von Bingen / arr: Monica Schley

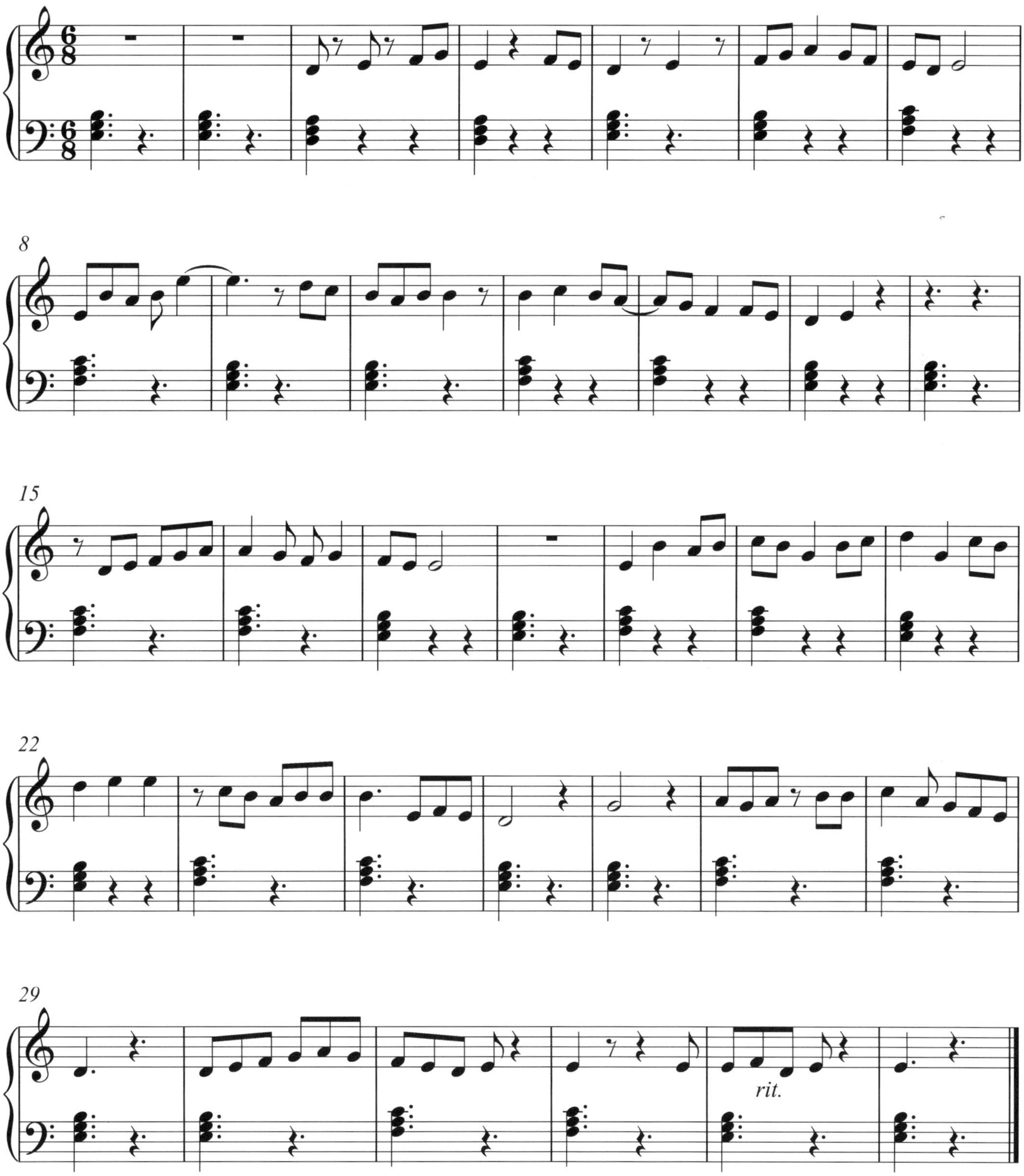

O Frondens Virga

arr: Monica Schley

Hildegard von Bingen

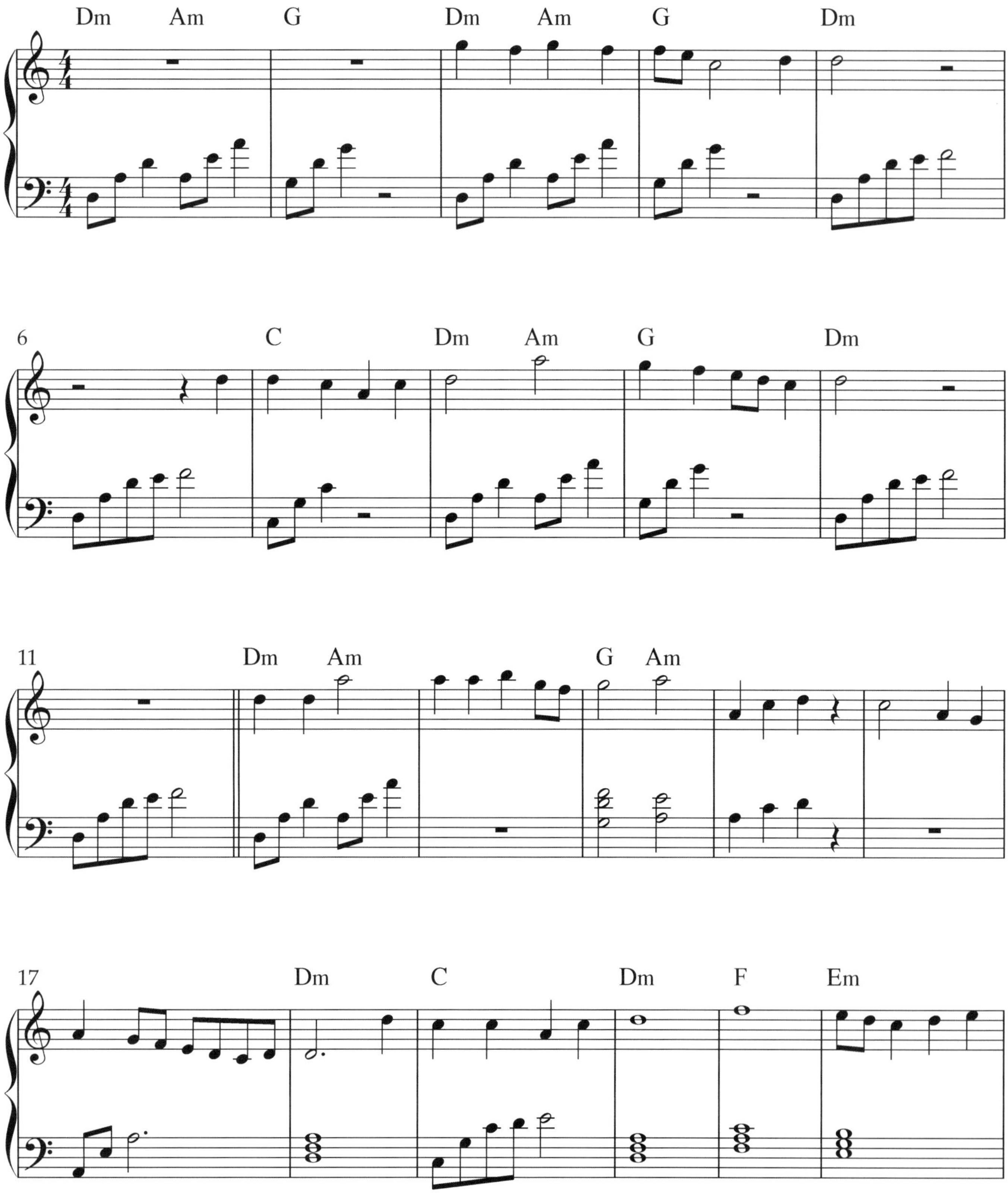

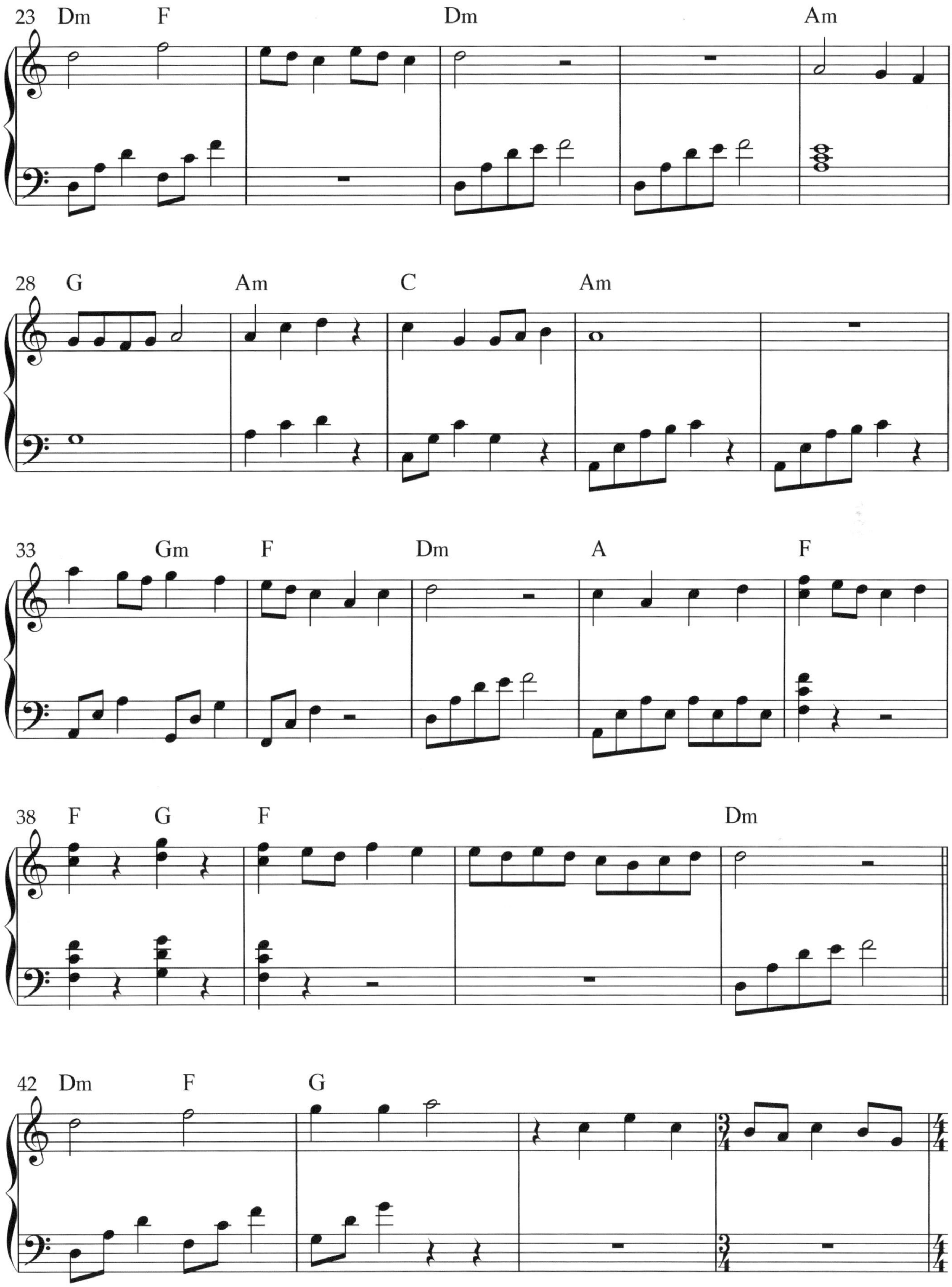
23 Dm F Dm Am
28 G Am C Am
33 Gm F Dm A F
38 F G F Dm
42 Dm F G

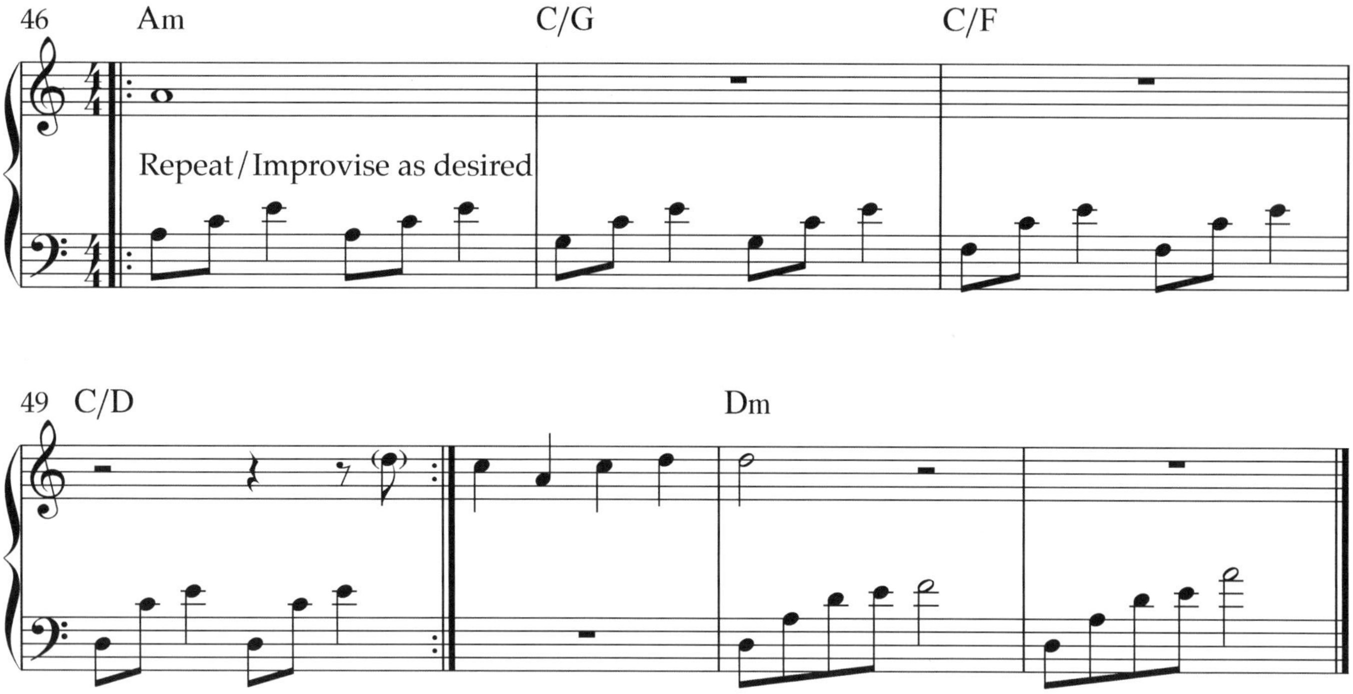
46
Am
C/G
C/F
Repeat/Improvise as desired
49
C/D
Dm

simplified for small harp

Deus Anim Rorem

arr: Monica Schley

Hildegard von Bingen

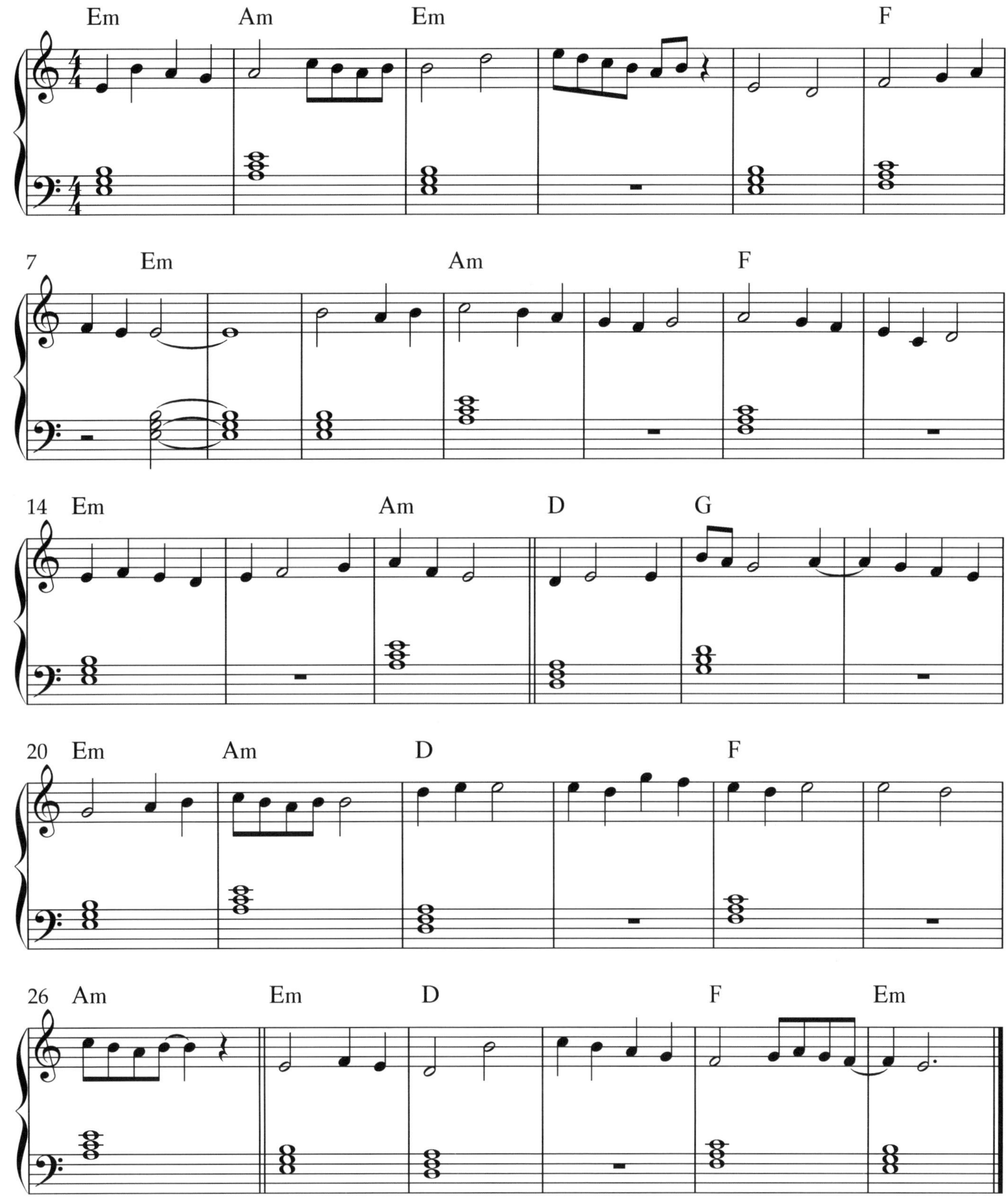

Deus Anim Rorem

arr: Monica Schley

Hildegard von Bingen

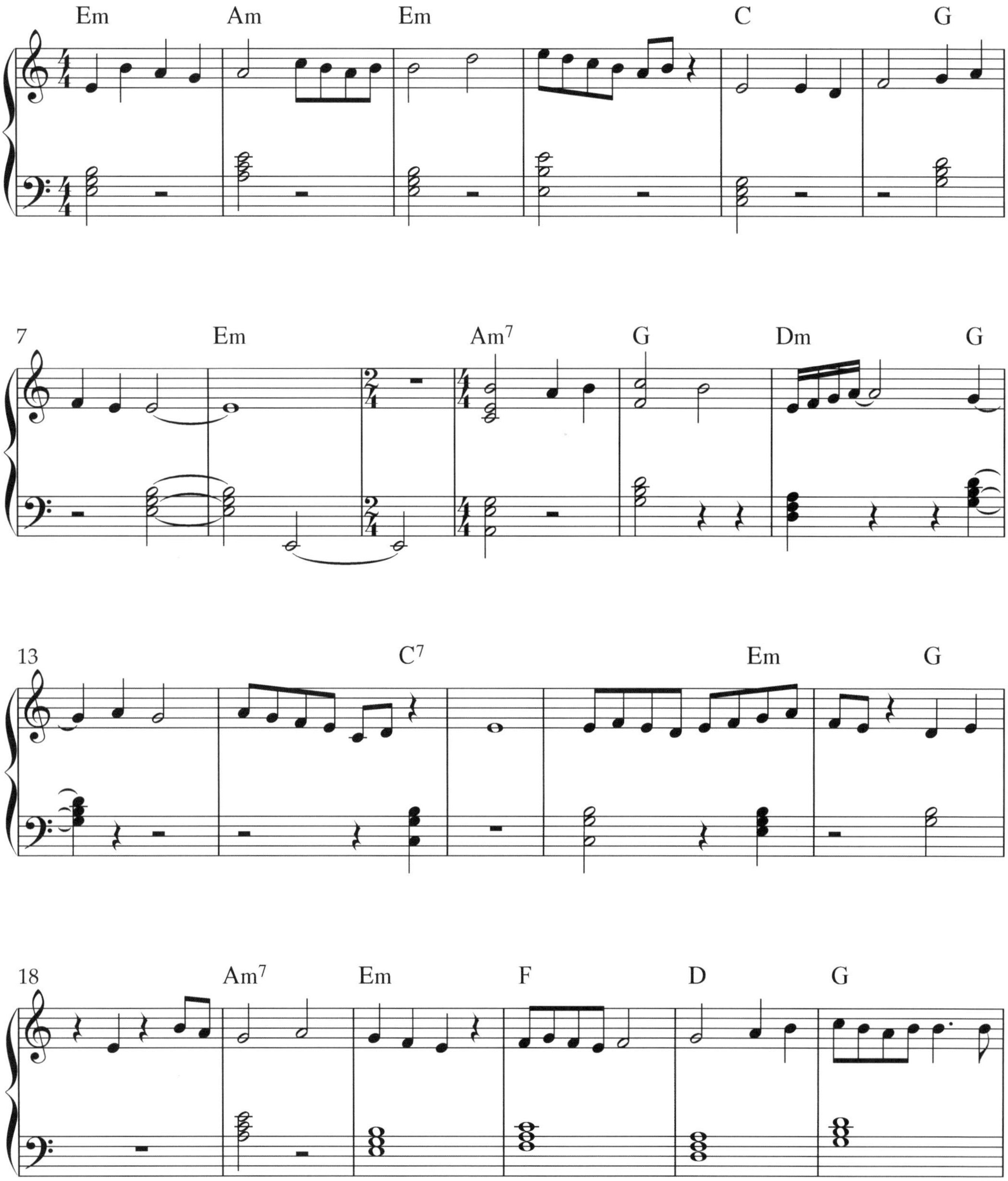

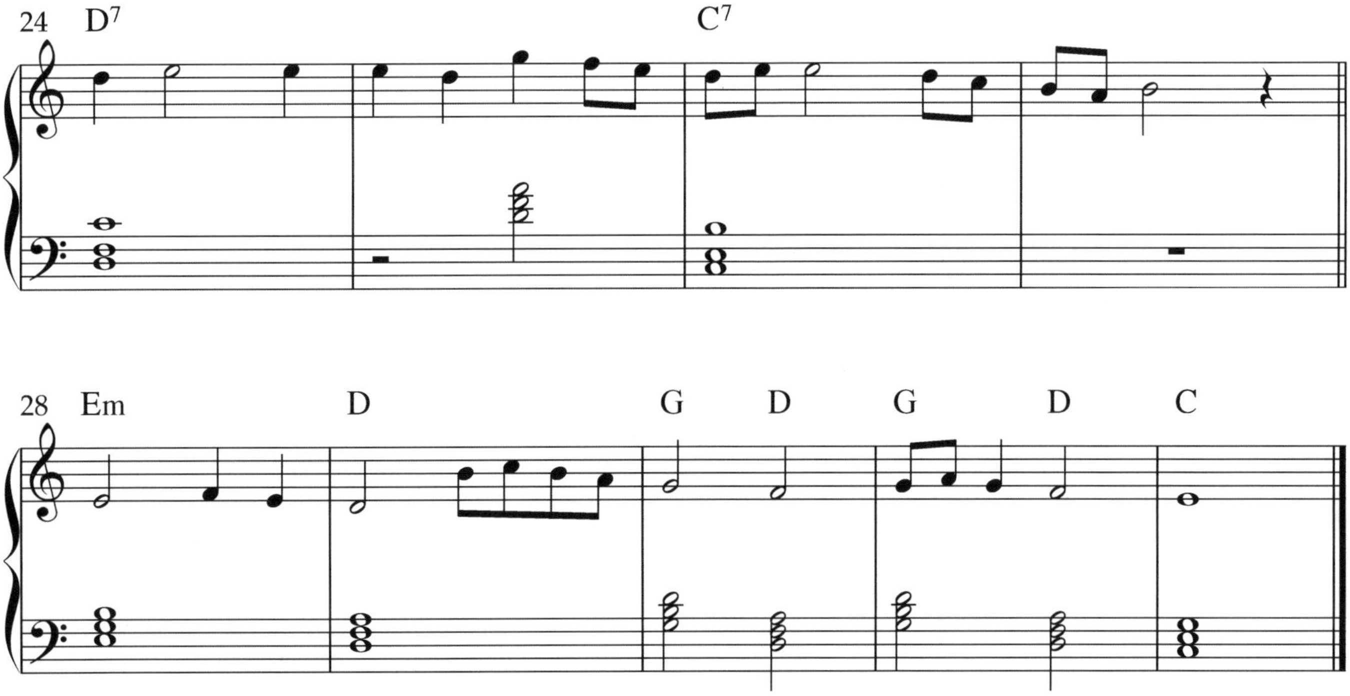
24
D7
C7
28
Em
D
G
D
G
D
C

simplified
for small harp

Deus Enim

arr: Monica Schley

Hildegard von Bingen

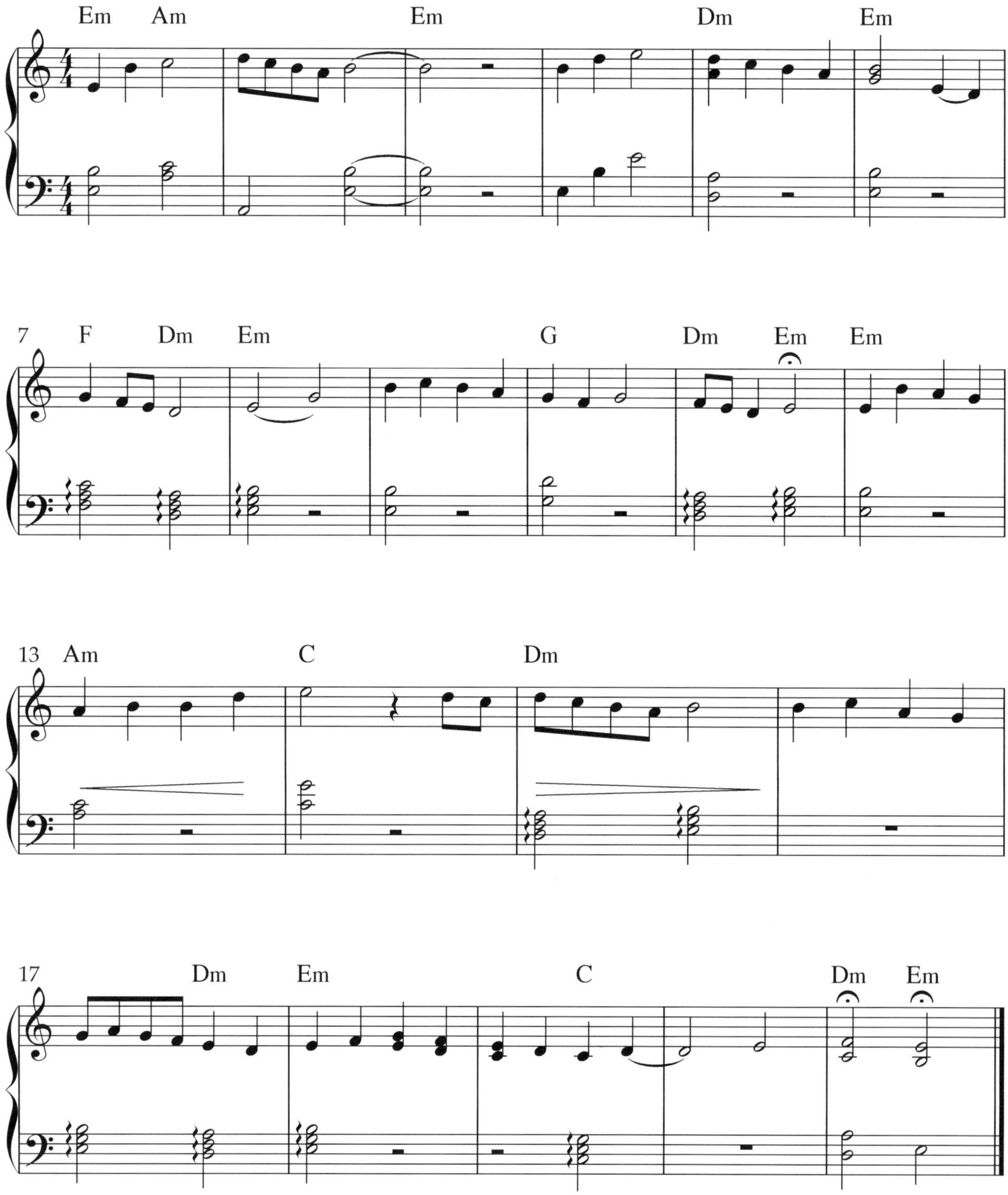

Deus Enim

arr: Monica Schley

Hildegard von Bingen

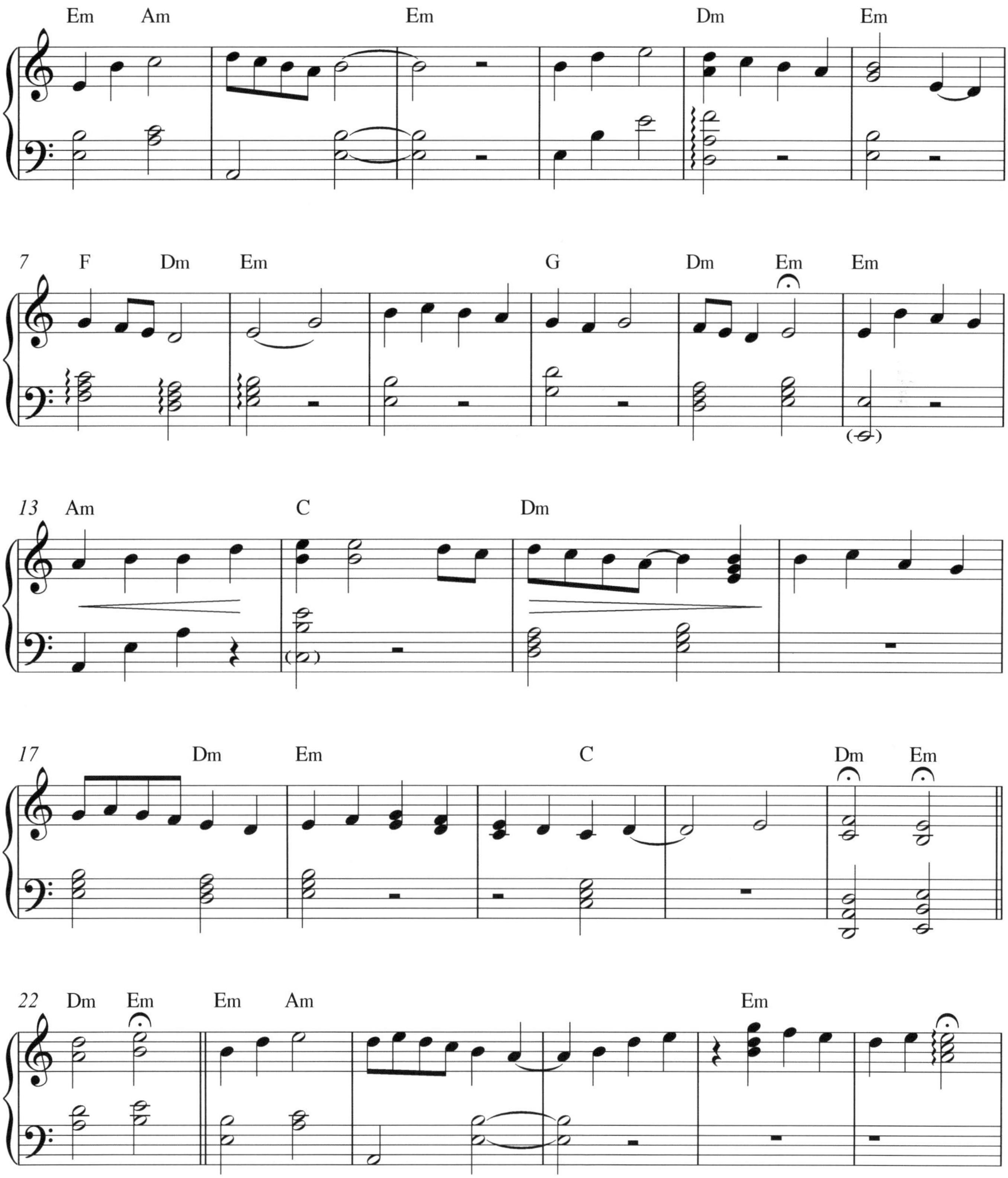

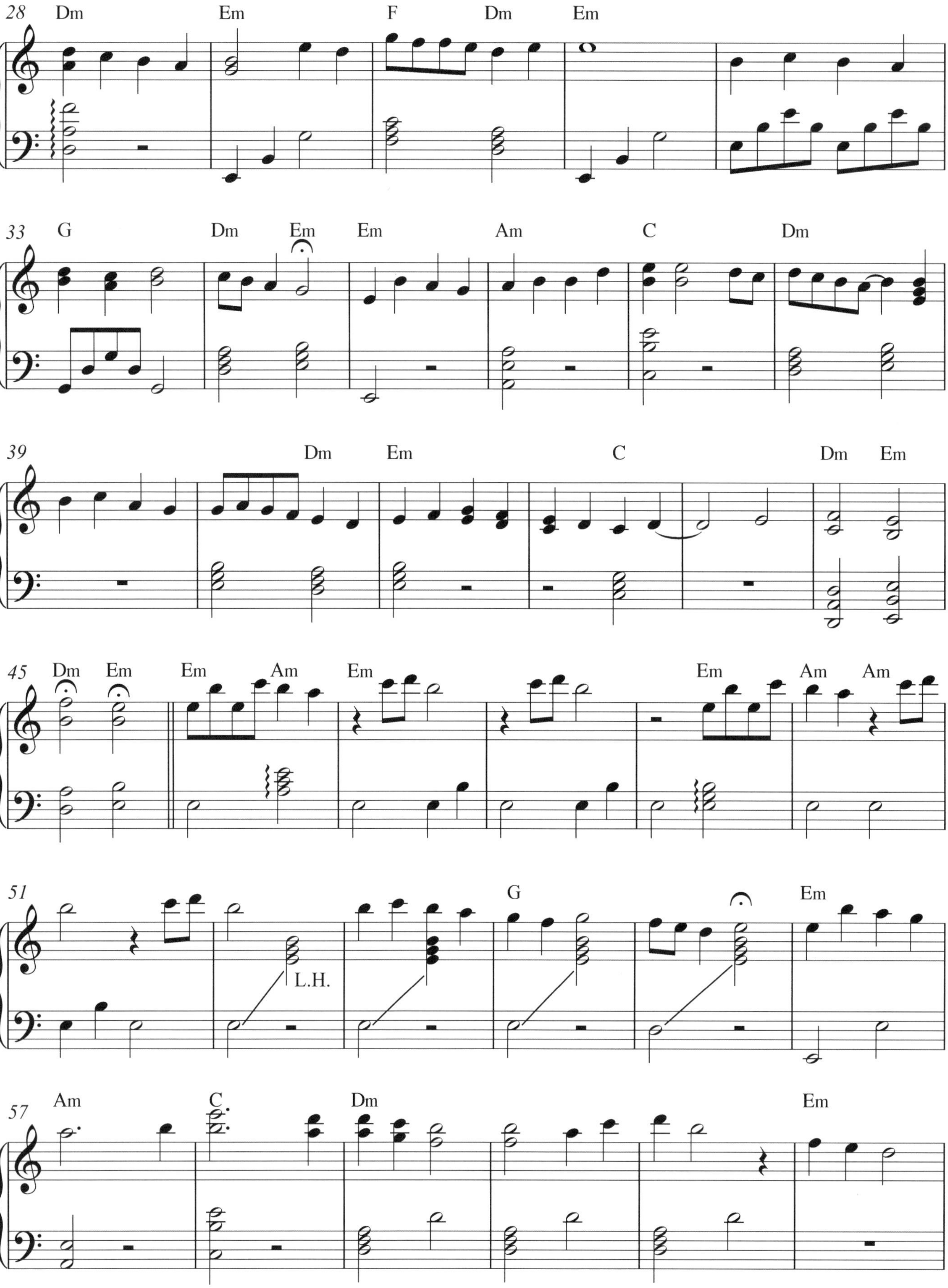
28
Dm
Em
F
Dm
Em
33
G
Dm
Em
Em
Am
C
Dm
39
Dm
Em
C
Dm
Em
45
Dm
Em
Em
Am
Em
Em
Am
Am
51
L.H.
G
Em
57
Am
C
Dm
Em

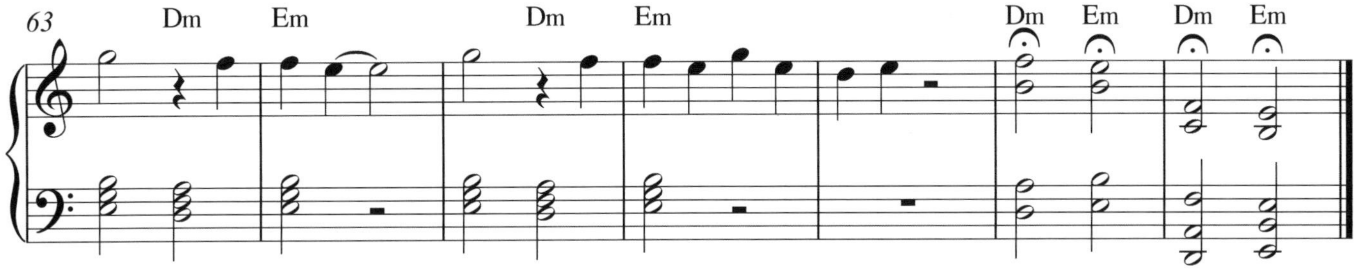
63
Dm
Em
Dm
Em
Dm
Em
Dm
Em

for small therapy harp

Unde Quocumque

arr: Monica Schley

Hildegard von Bingen

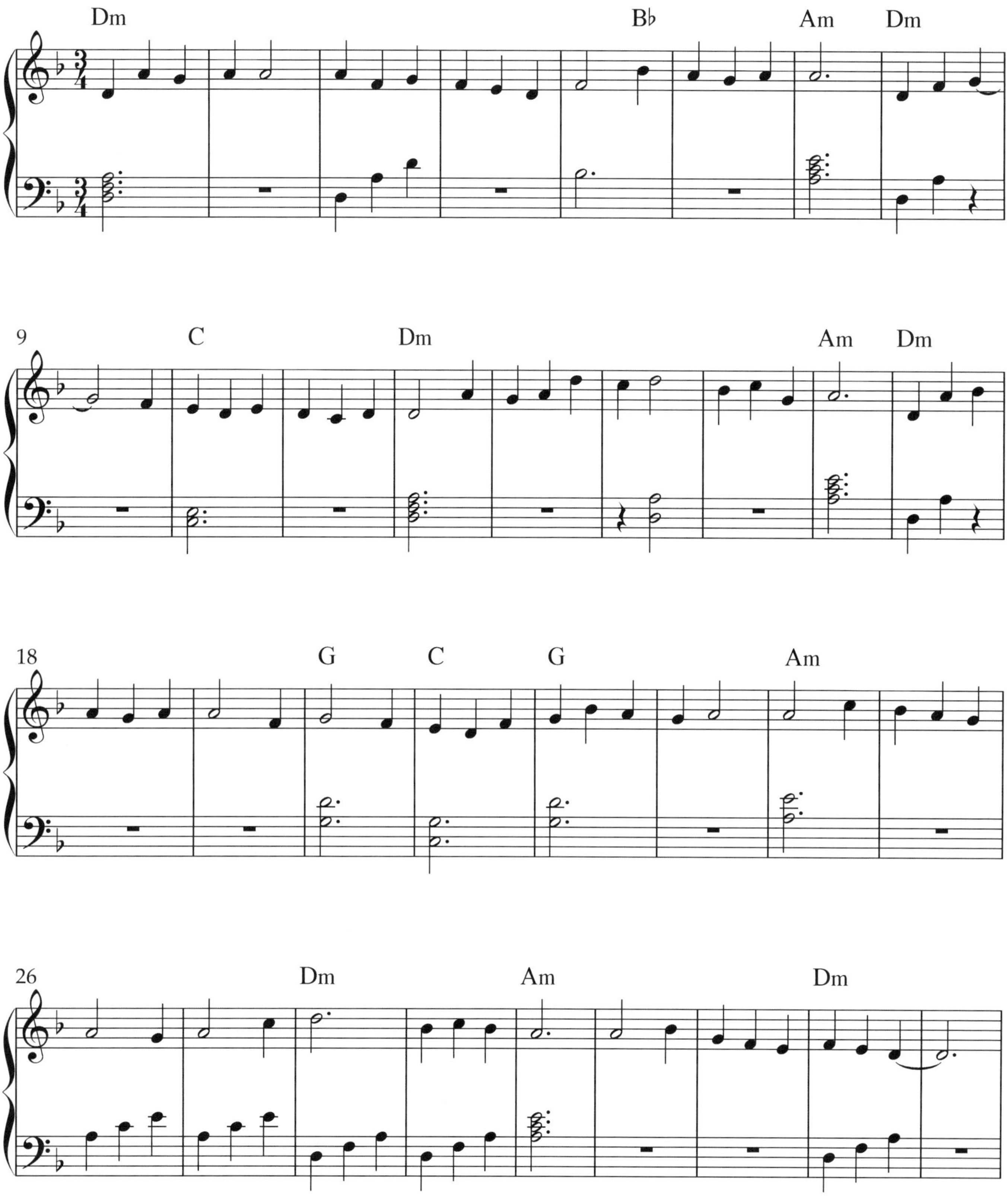

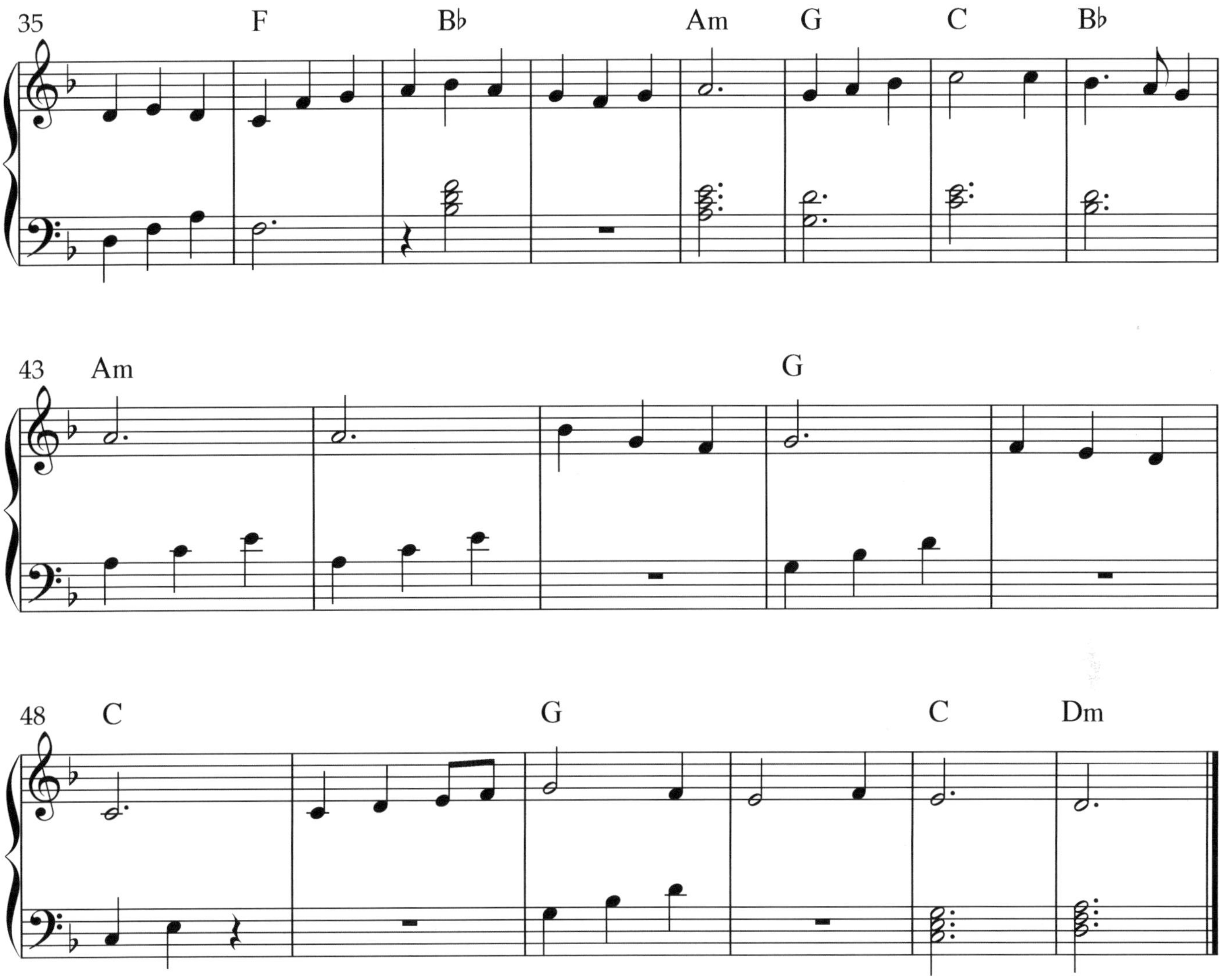
35
F
B♭
Am
G
C
B♭
43
Am
G
48
C
G
C
Dm

Unde Quocumque

arr: Monica Schley

Hildegard von Bingen

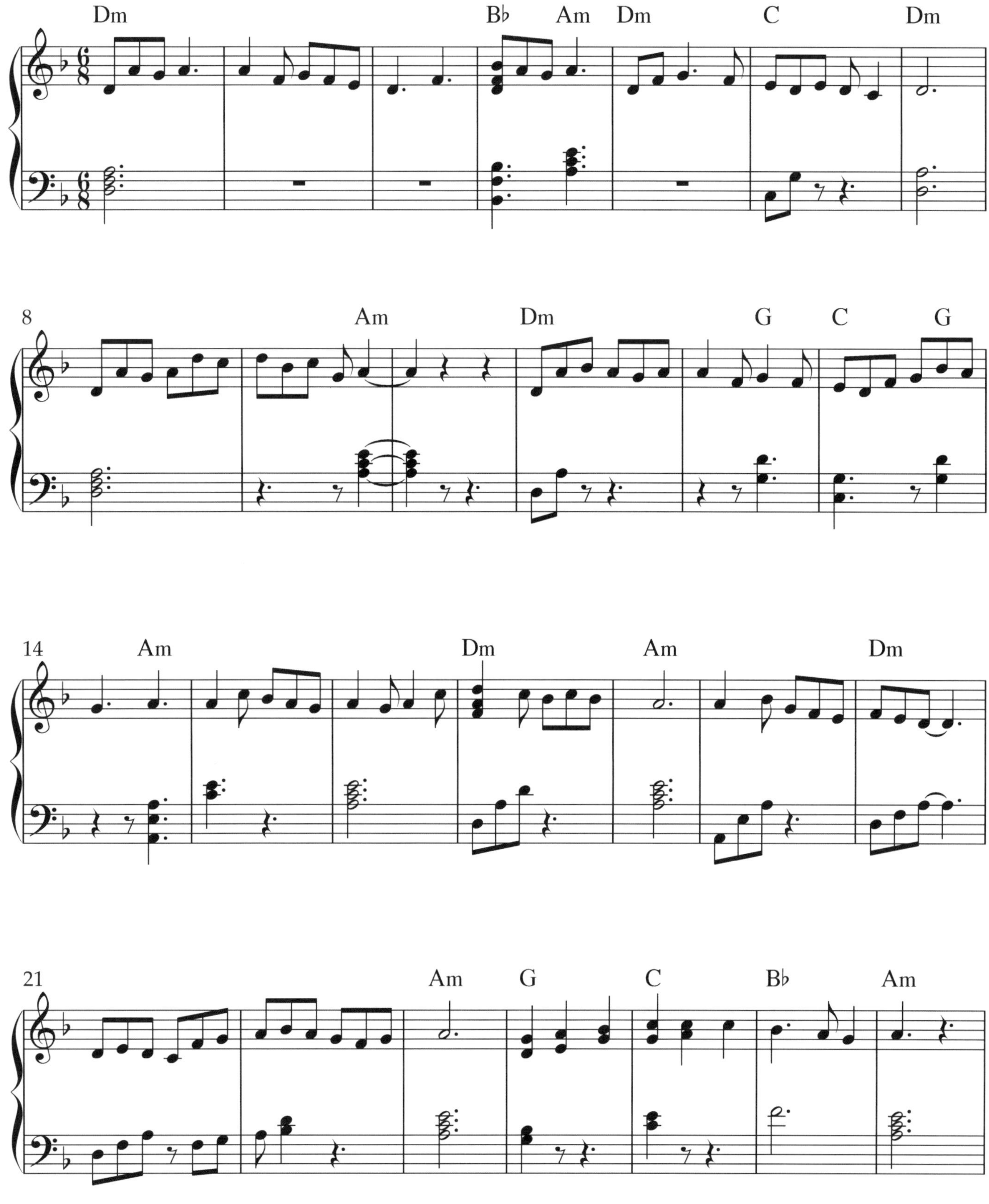

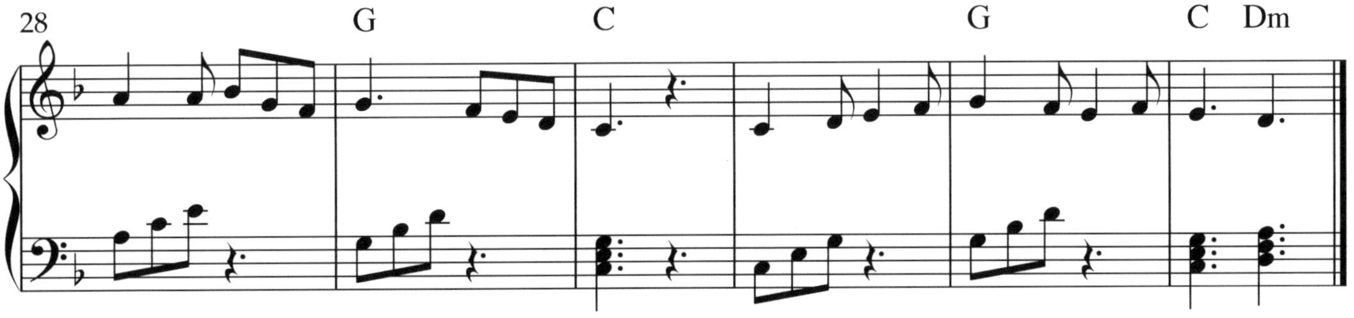
28
G
C
G
C Dm

O Cruror Sanguinis

arr: Monica Schley

Hildegard von Bingen

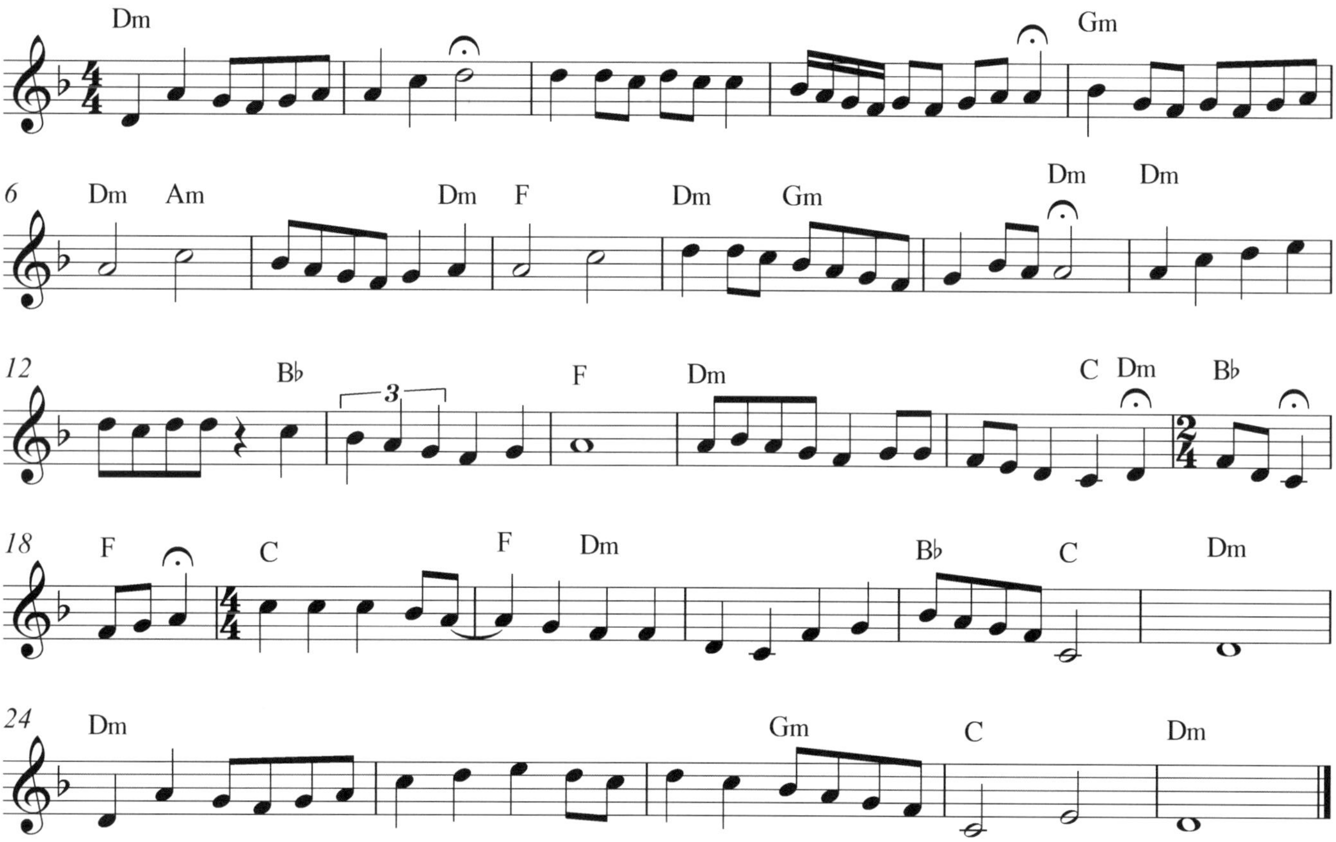

This page has been left blank to avoid an awkward page turn.

O Cruor Sanguinis

arr: Monica Schley

Hildegard von Bingen

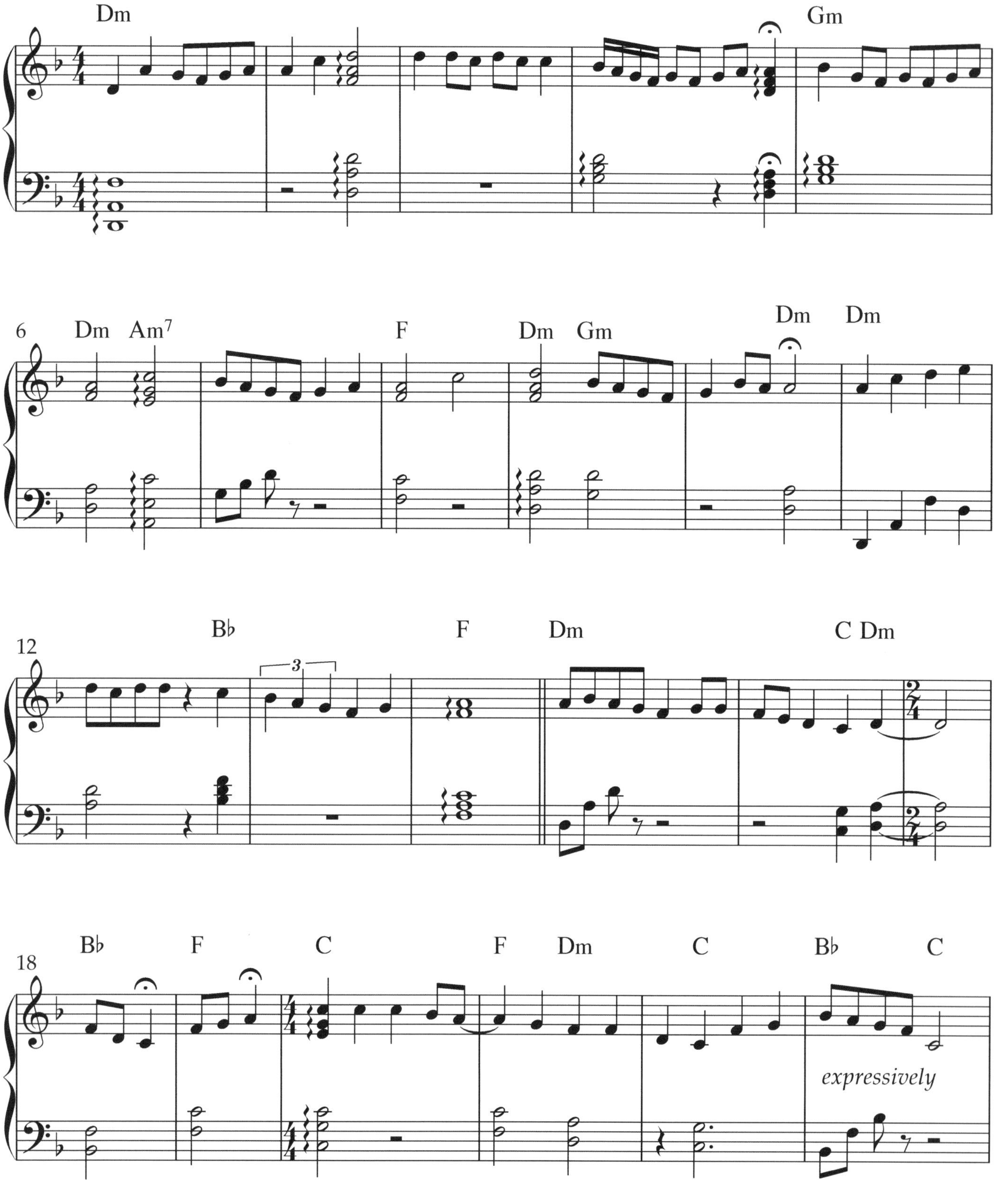

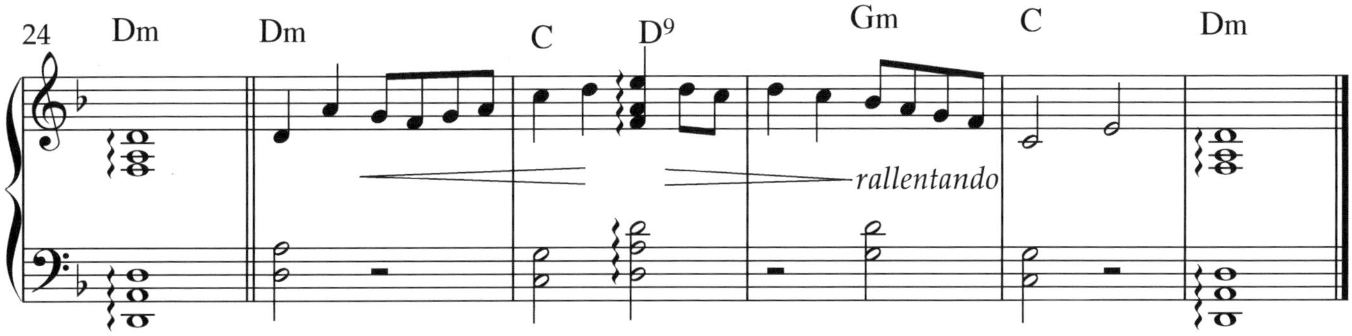
24
Dm
Dm
C
D9
Gm
C
Dm
rallentando

Et Ideo

arr: Monica Schley

Hildegard von Bingen

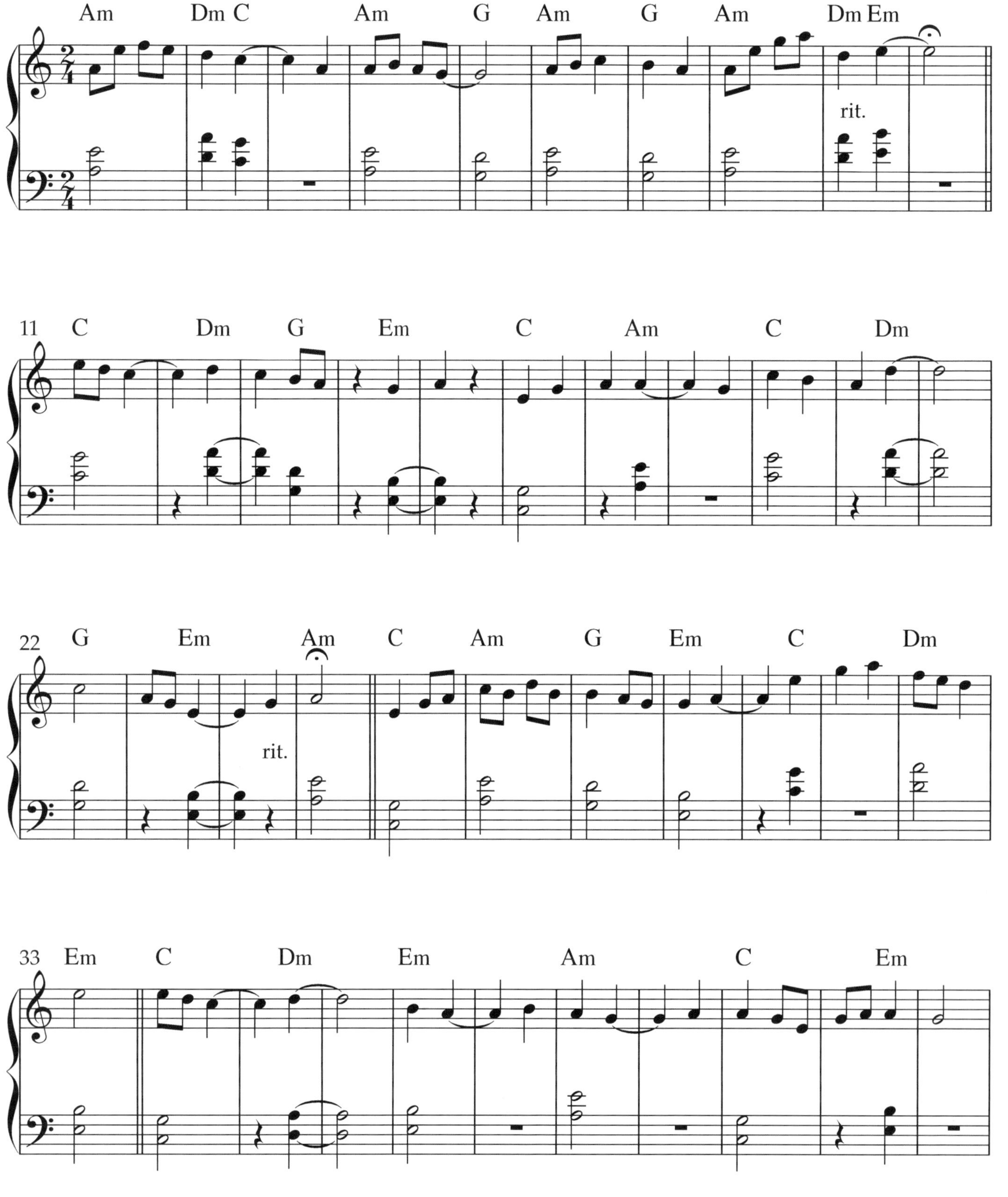

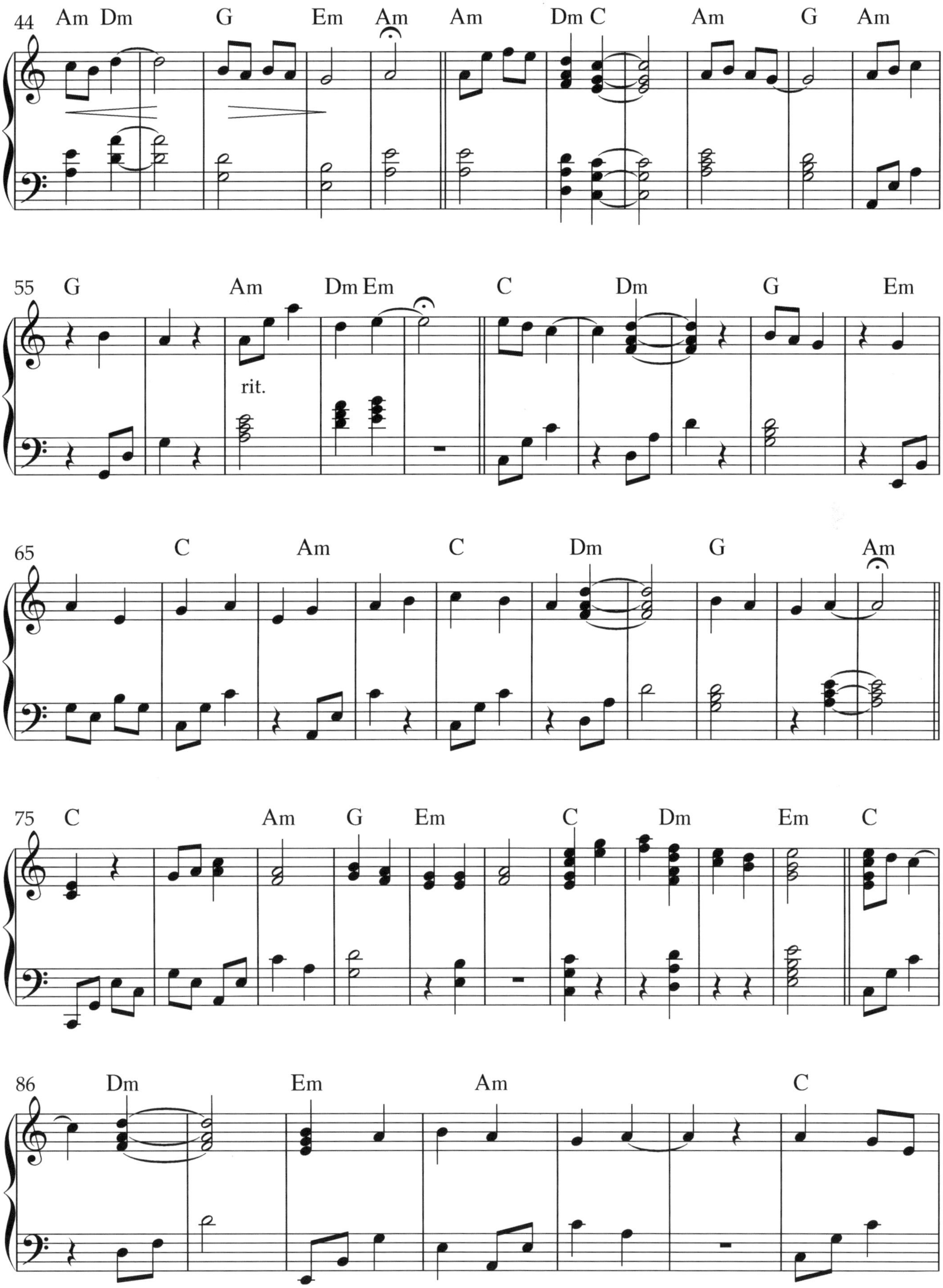
44
Am Dm G Em Am Am Dm C Am G Am
55
G Am Dm Em C Dm G Em
rit.
65
C Am C Dm G Am
75
C Am G Em C Dm Em C
86
Dm Em Am C

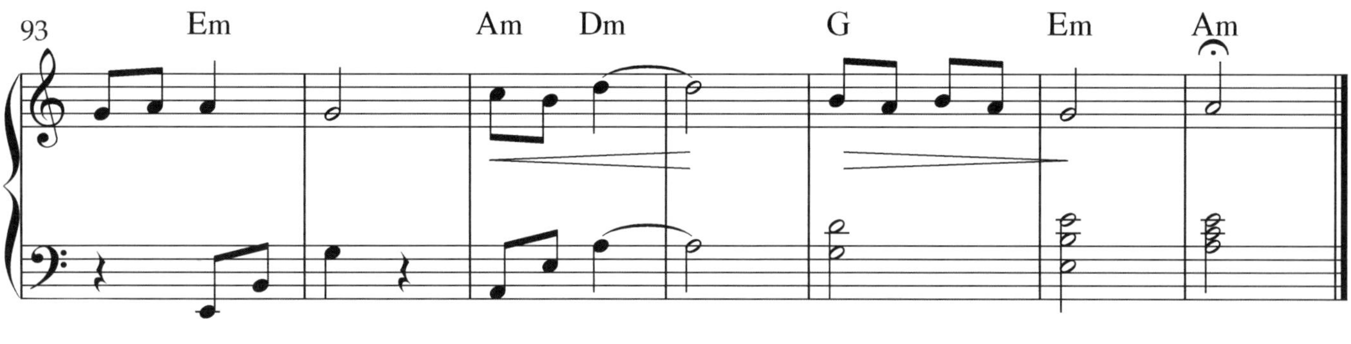
93
Em
Am
Dm
G
Em
Am

This page has been left blank to avoid an awkward page turn.

Levers: Set 3rd Oct B♭

De Patria

arr: Monica Schley

Hildegard von Bingen

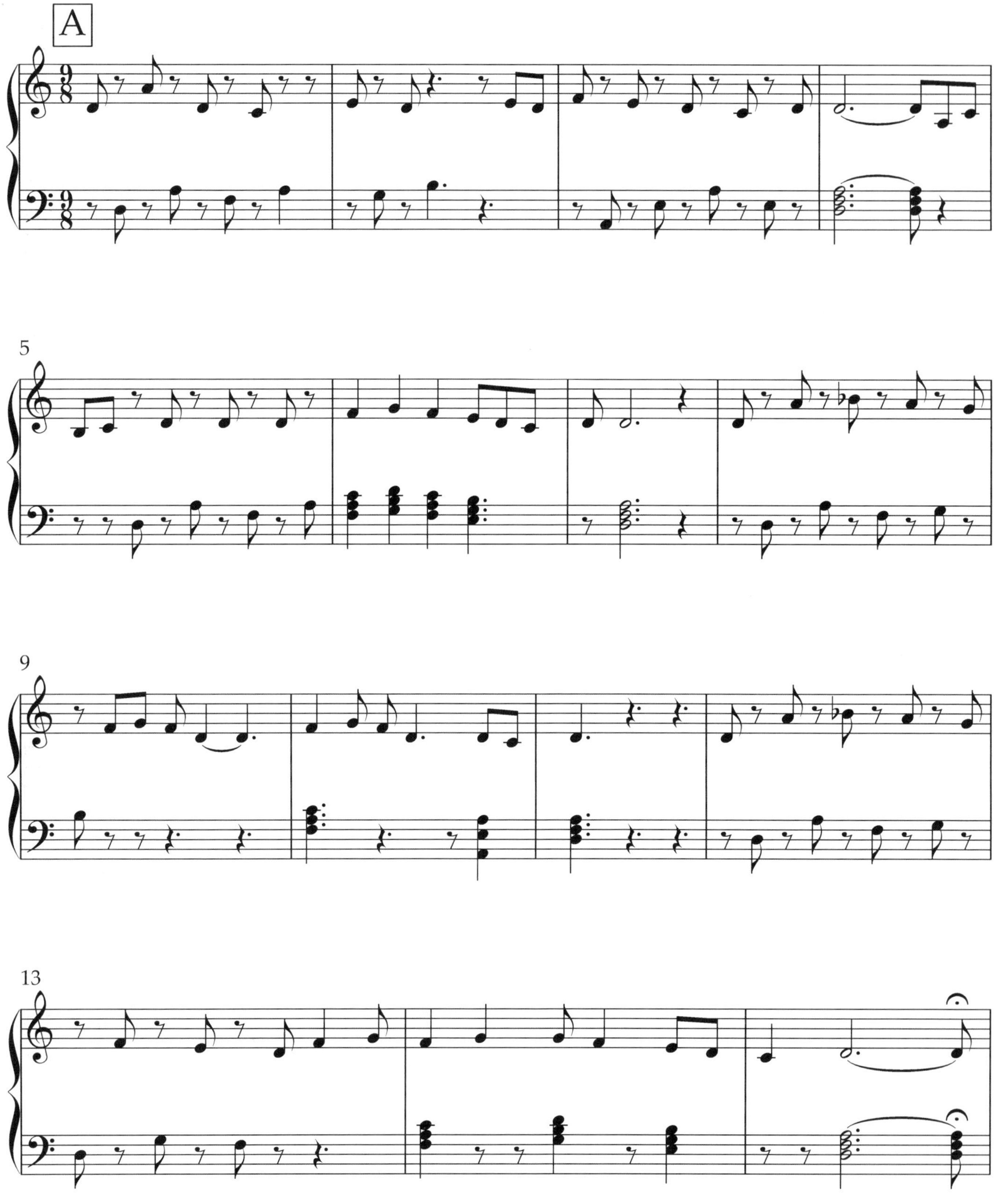

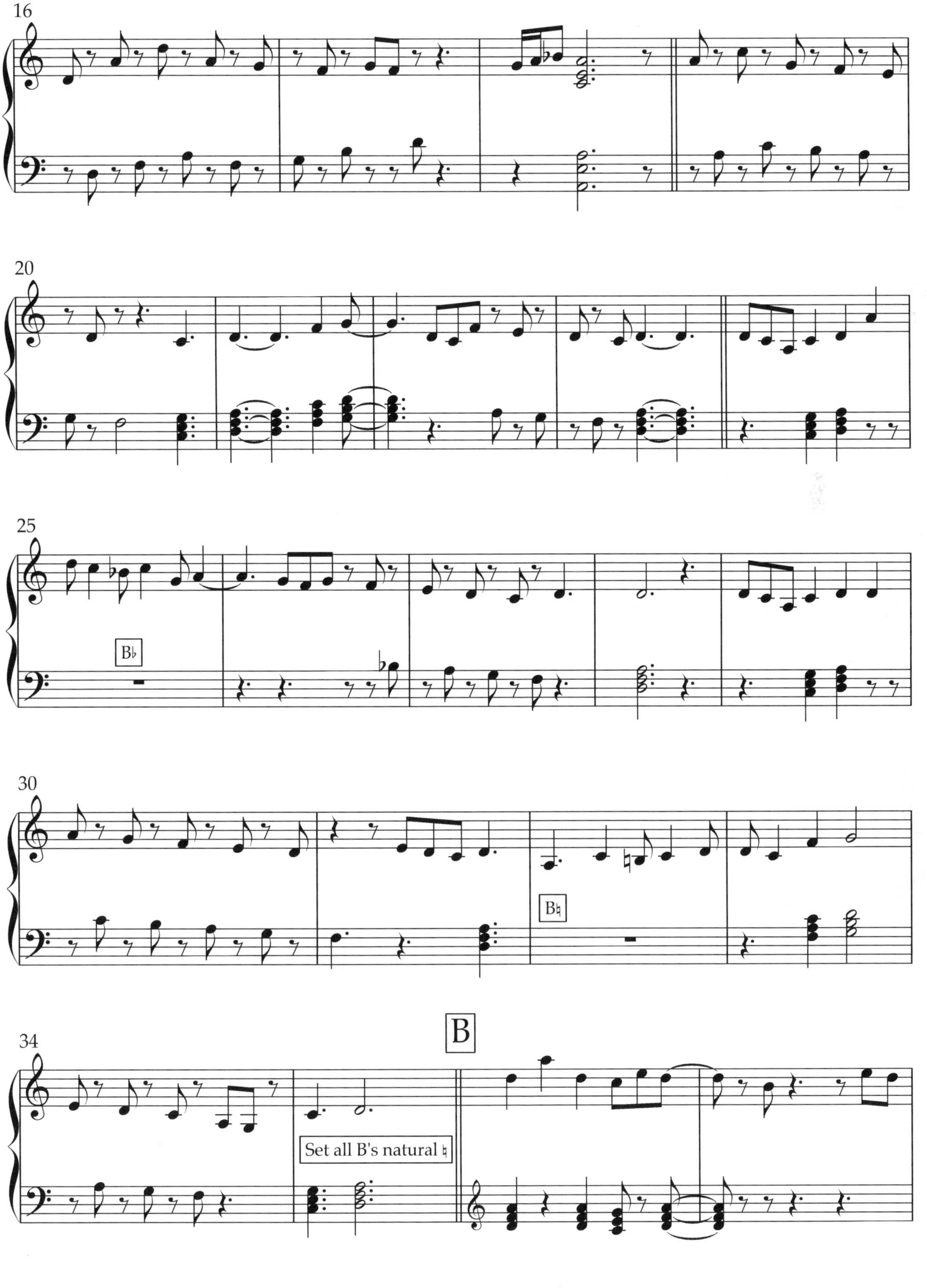
16
20
25
B♭
30
B♮
34
B
Set all B's natural ♮

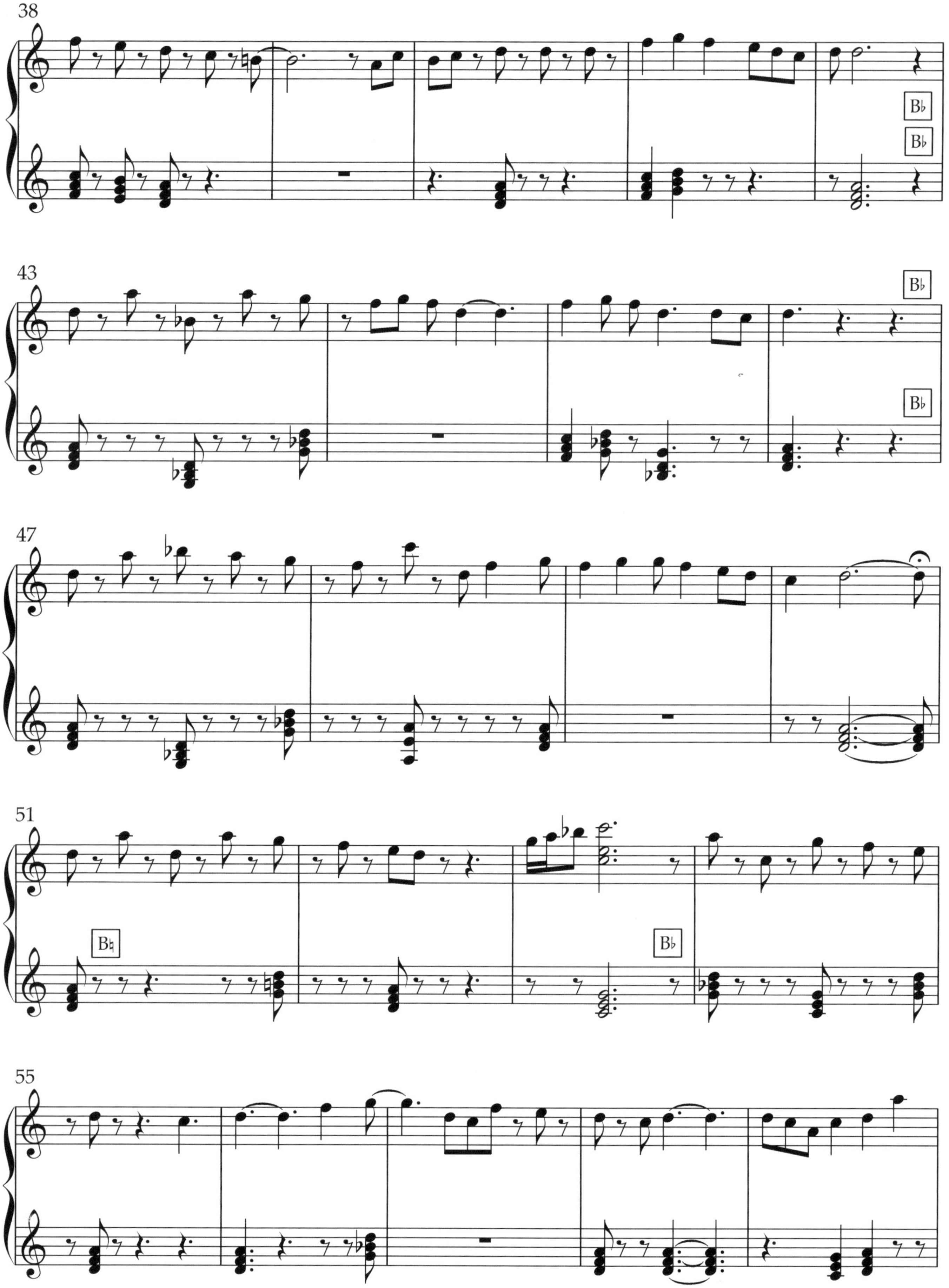
38
B♭
B♭
43
B♭
B♭
47
51
B♮
B♭
55

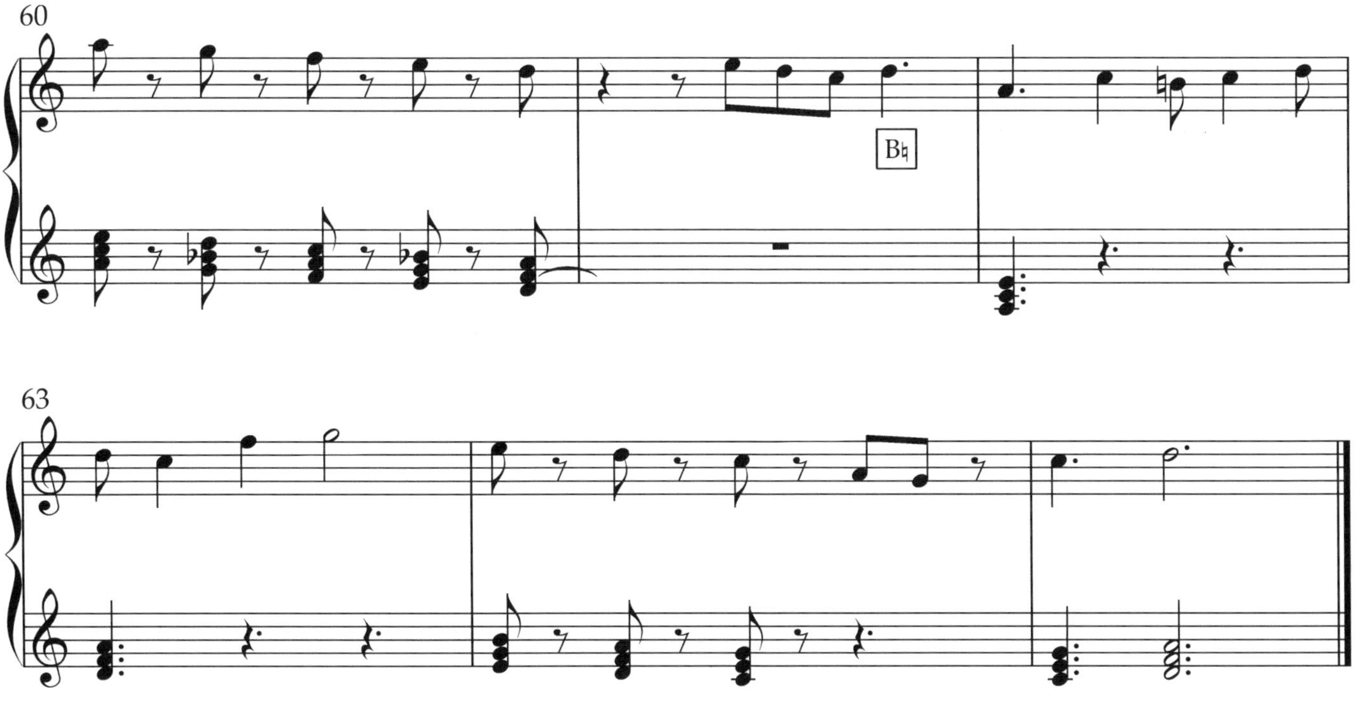
60
B♮
63

Sed Diabolus

arr: Monica Schley

Hildegard von Bingen

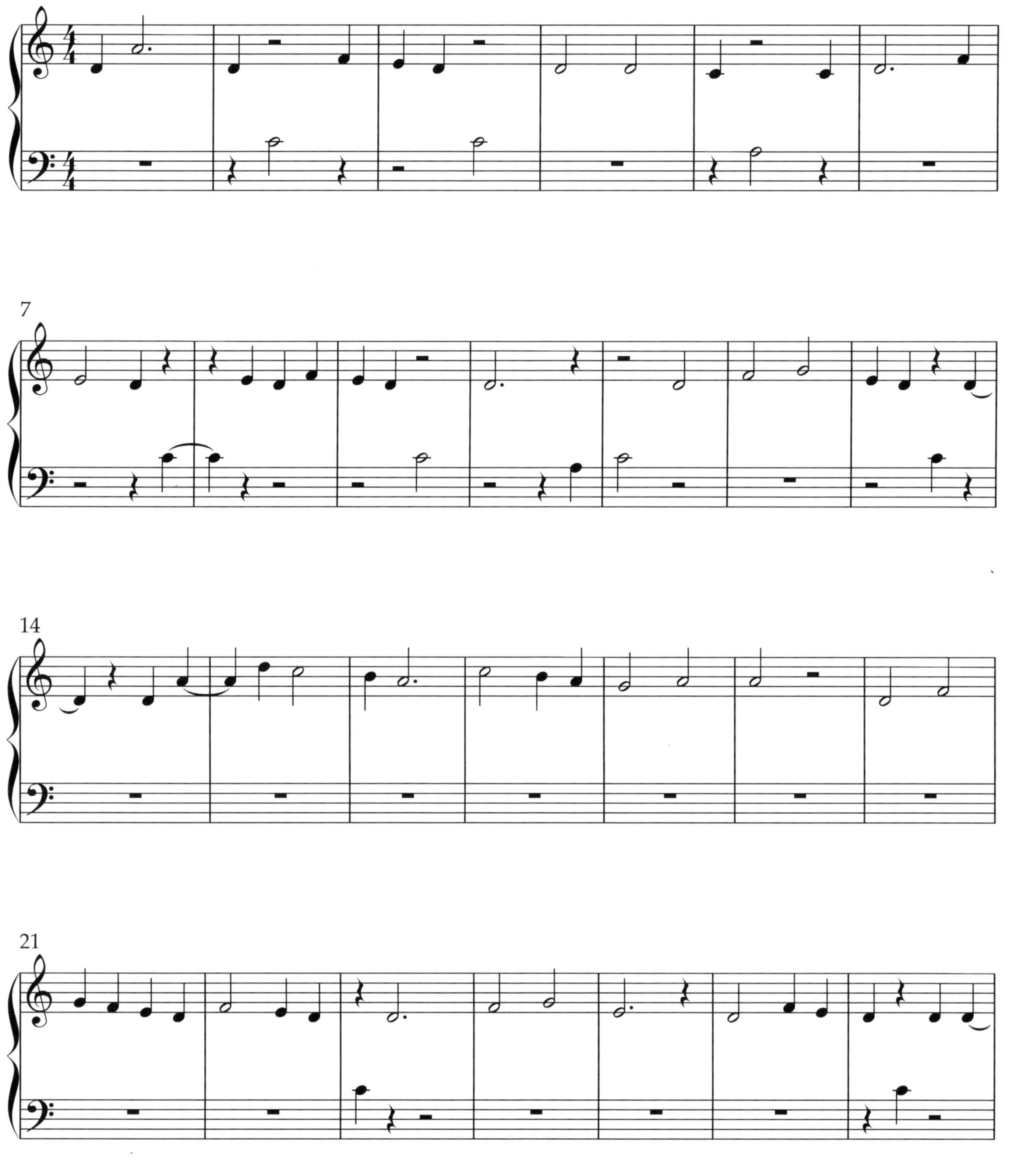

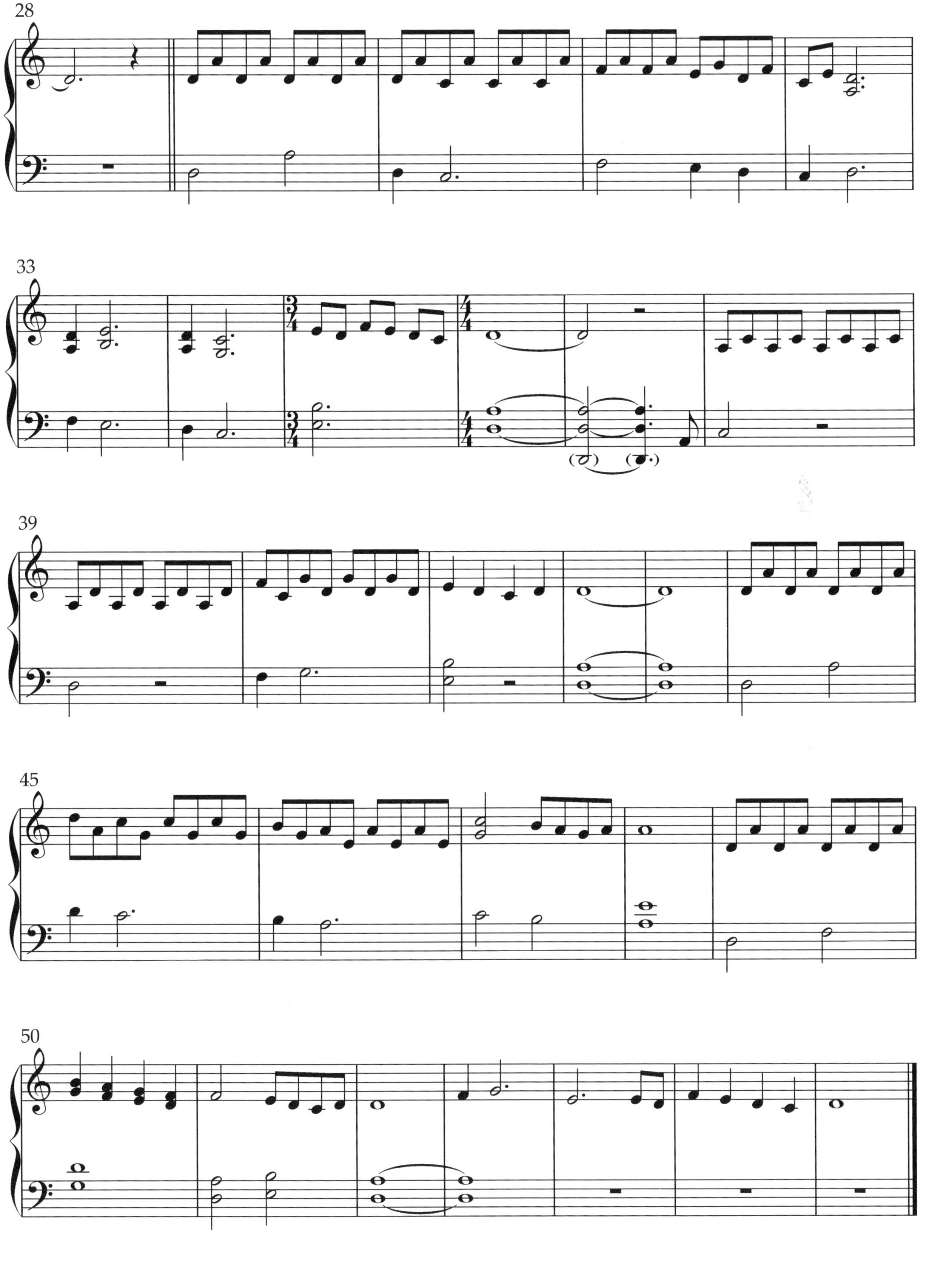
28
33
3/4
4/4
39
45
50

Studium Divinitatis

arr: Monica Schley

Hildegard von Bingen

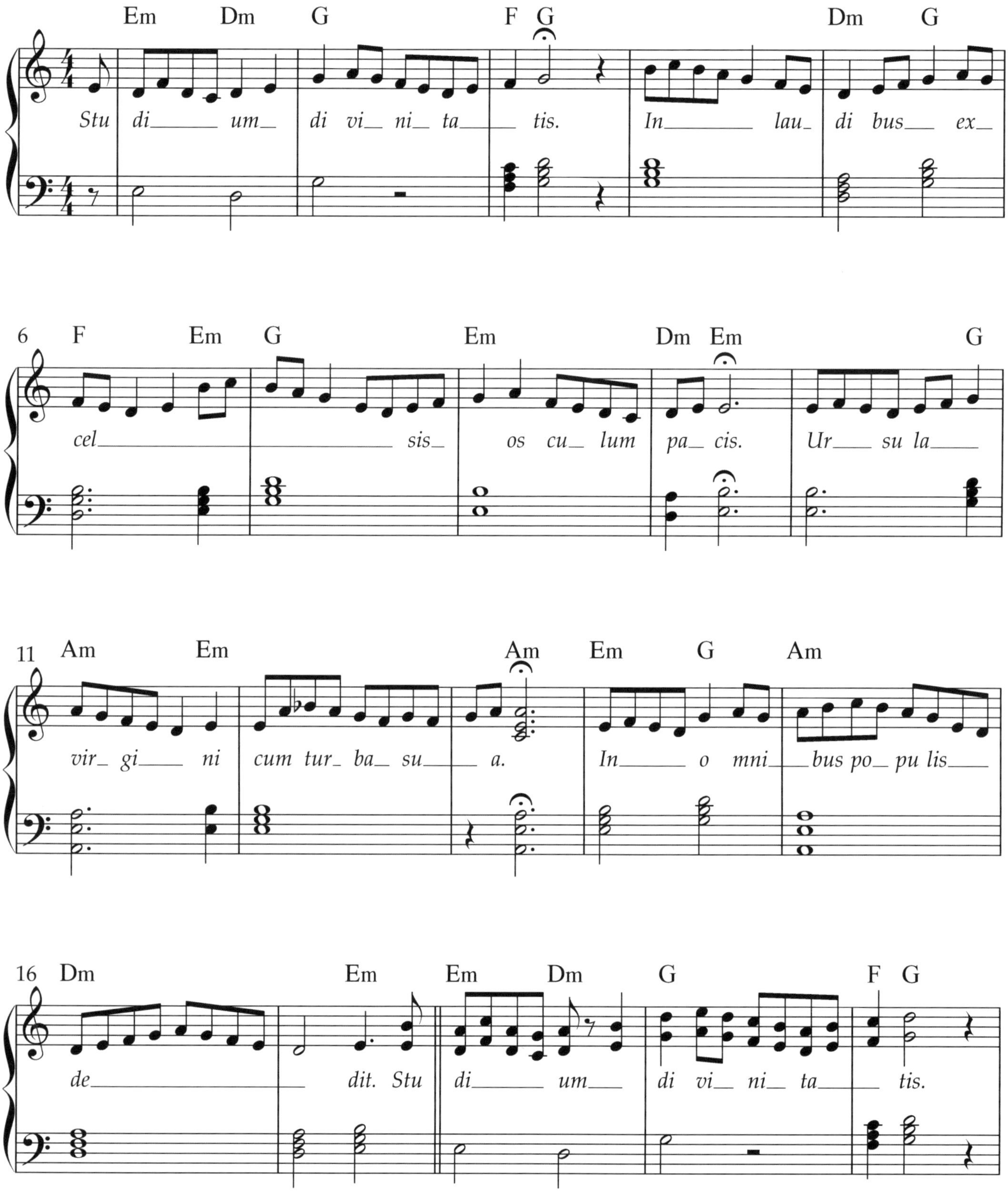

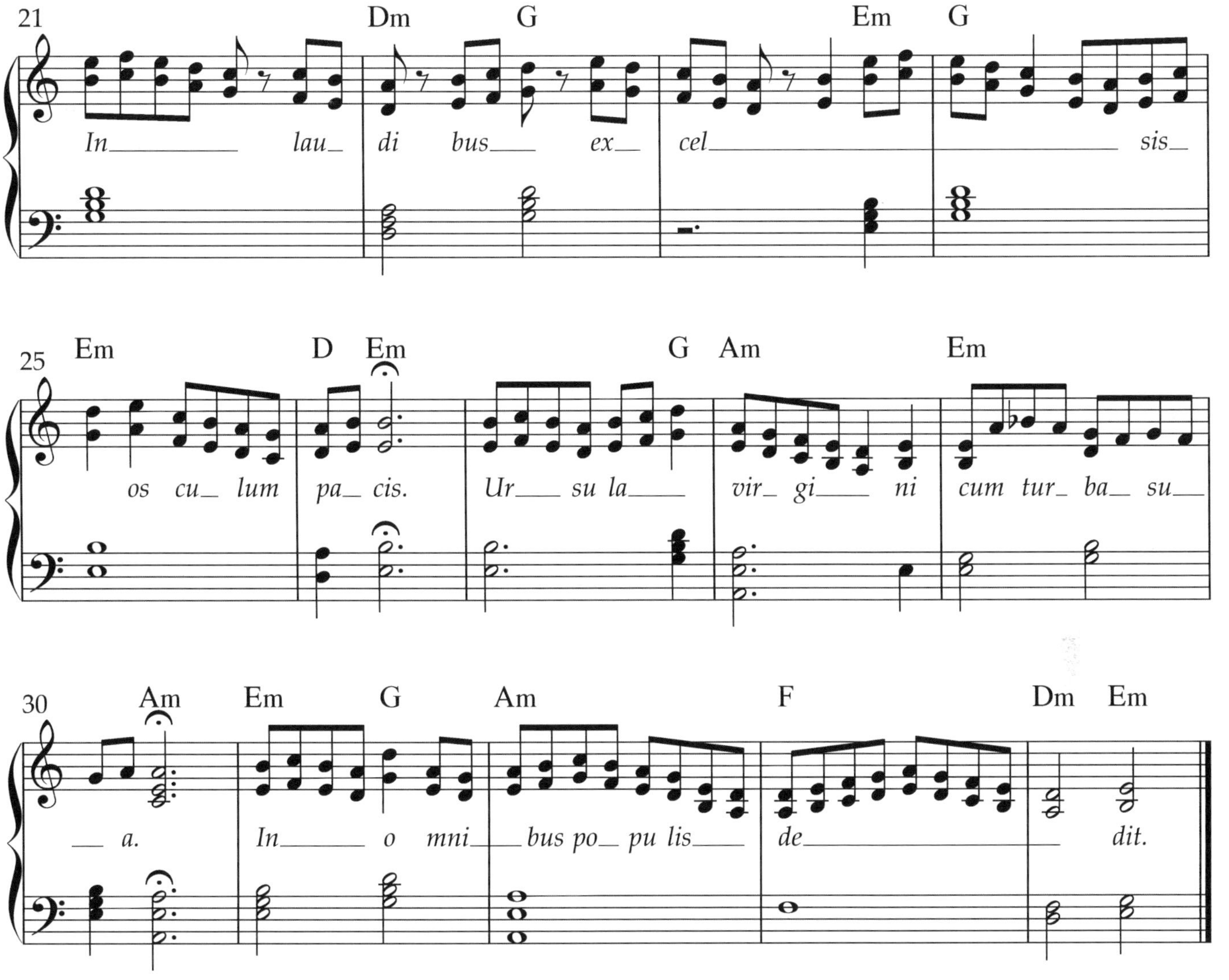
21
Dm G Em G
In lau_ di bus ex_ cel sis_
25
Em D Em G Am Em
os cu_ lum pa_ cis. Ur_ su la_ vir_ gi_ ni cum tur_ ba_ su_
30
Am Em G Am F Dm Em
a. In o mni bus po_ pu lis de dit.

O Virtus Sapientiae

15

arr: Monica Schley

Hildegard von Bingen

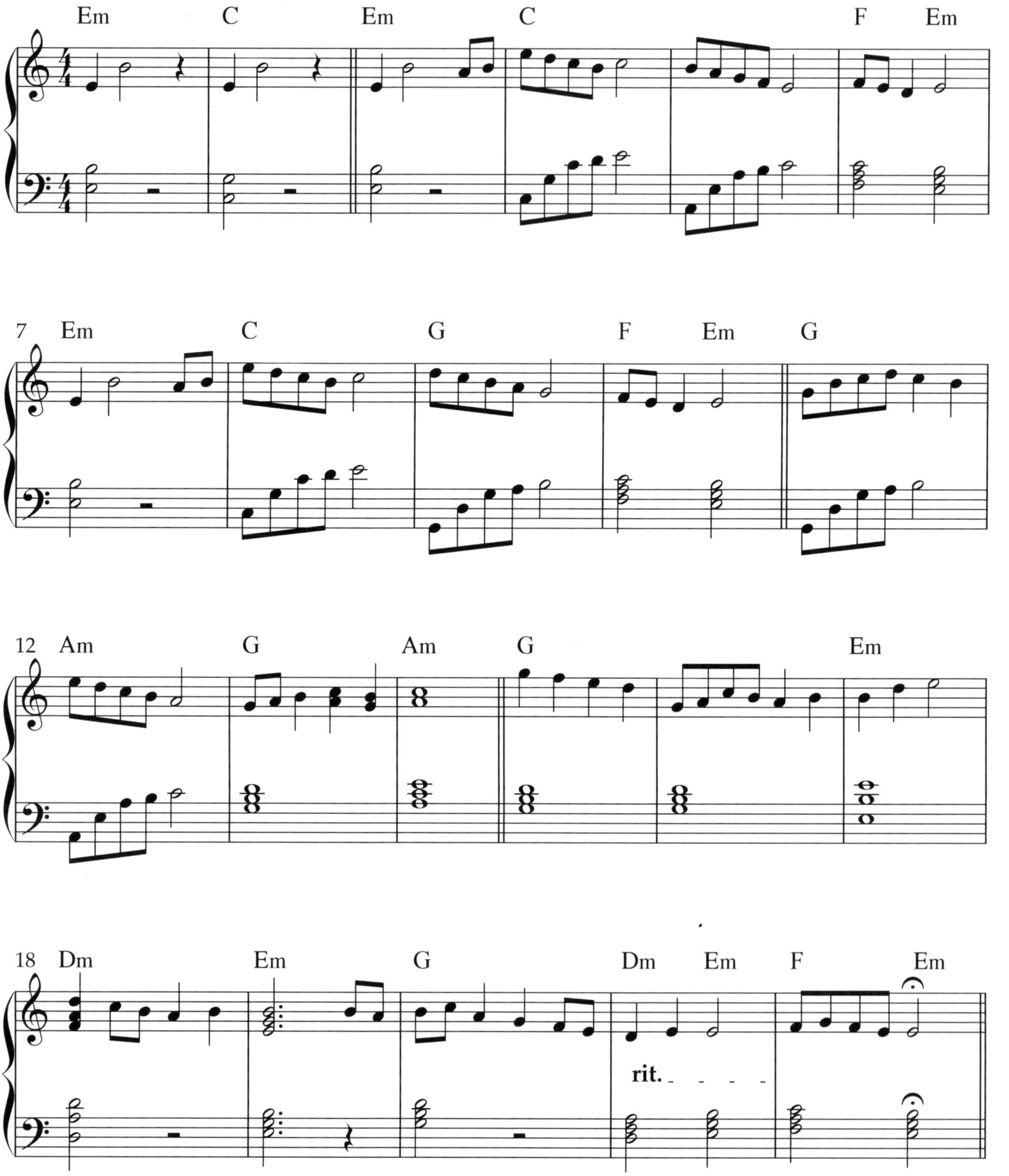

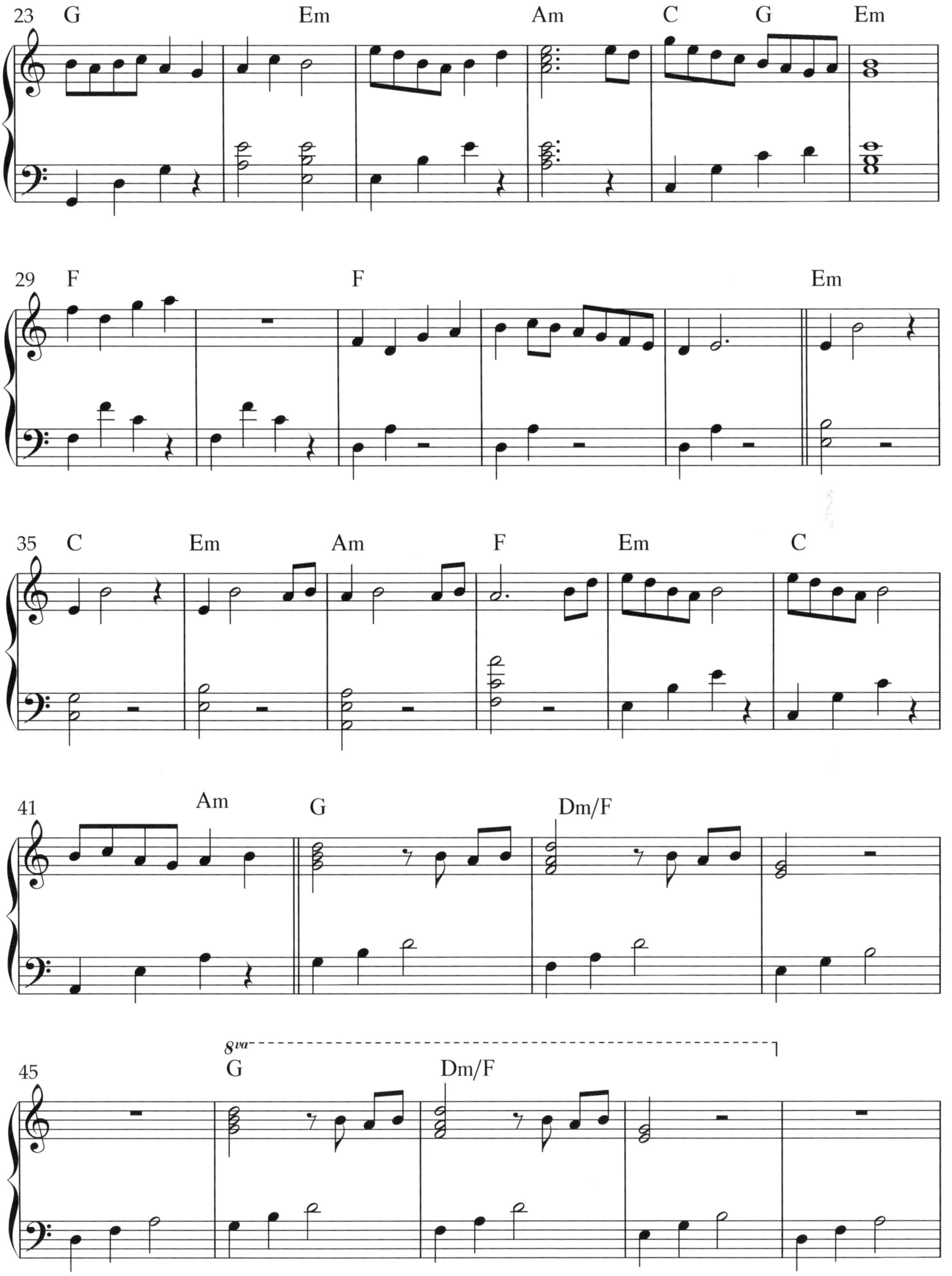
23
G
Em
Am
C
G
Em
29
F
F
Em
35
C
Em
Am
F
Em
C
41
Am
G
Dm/F
45
8va
G
Dm/F

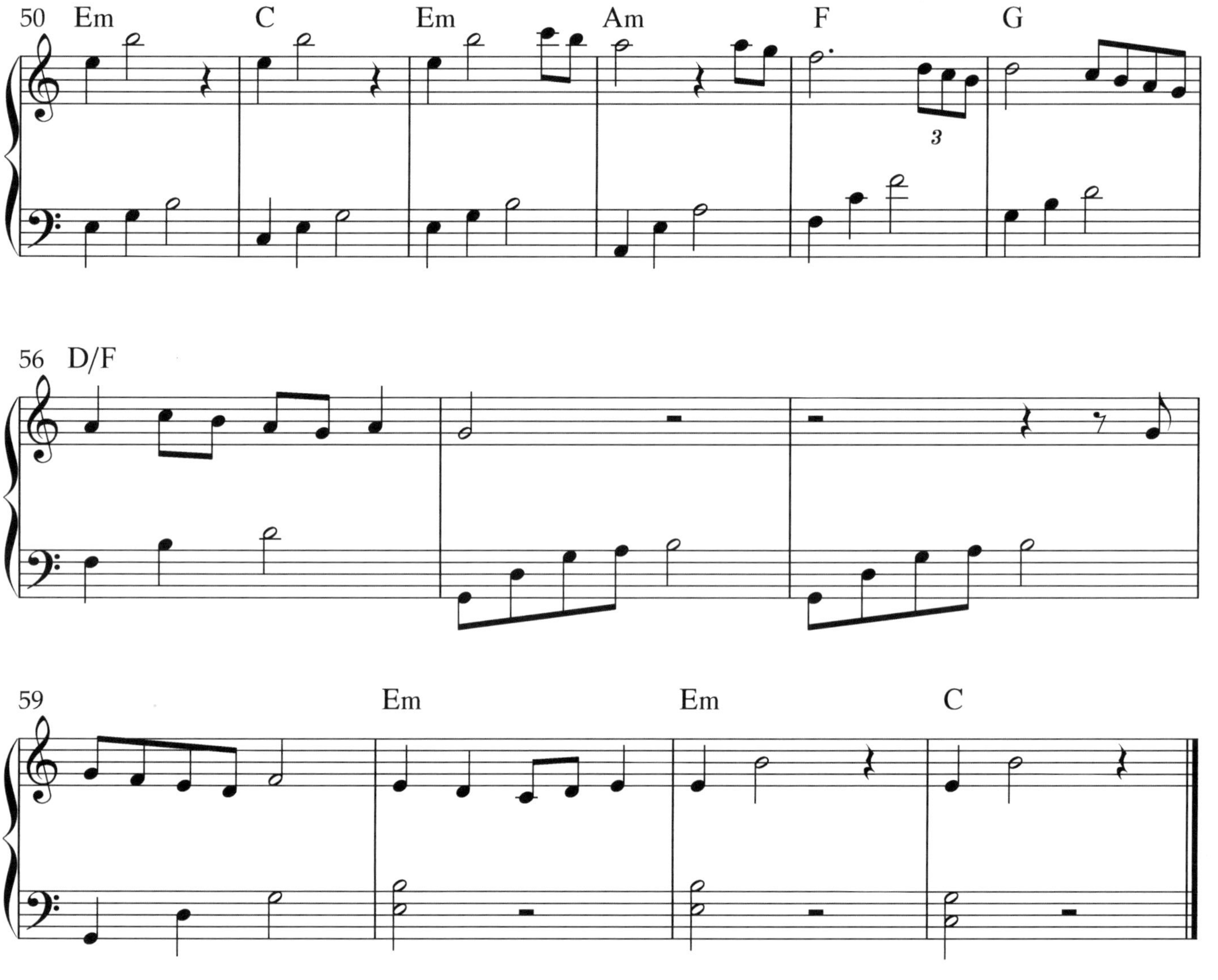
50 Em C Em Am F G
3
56 D/F
59 Em Em C

O Paster Animarum

16

arr: Monica Schley

Hildegard von Bingen

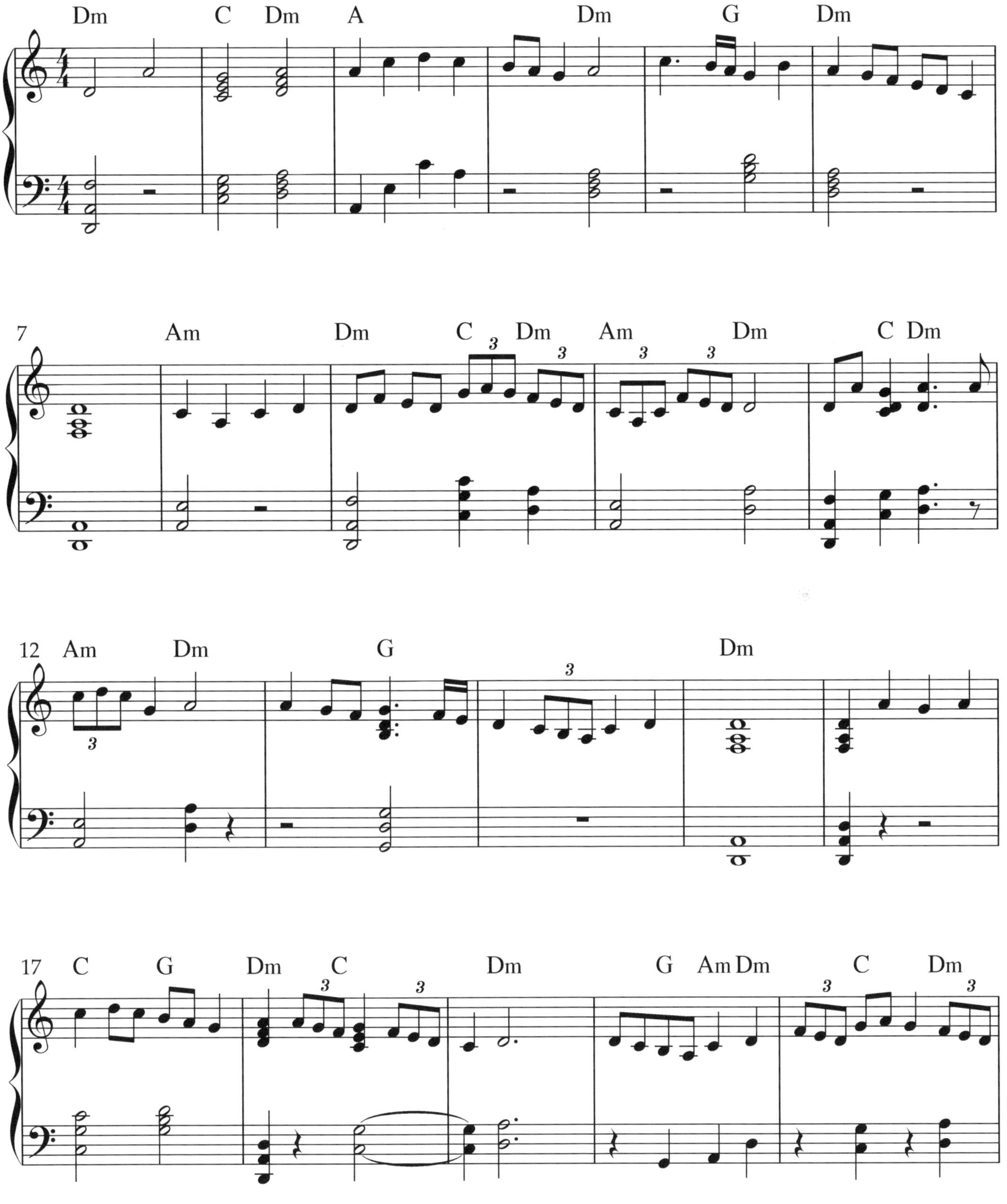

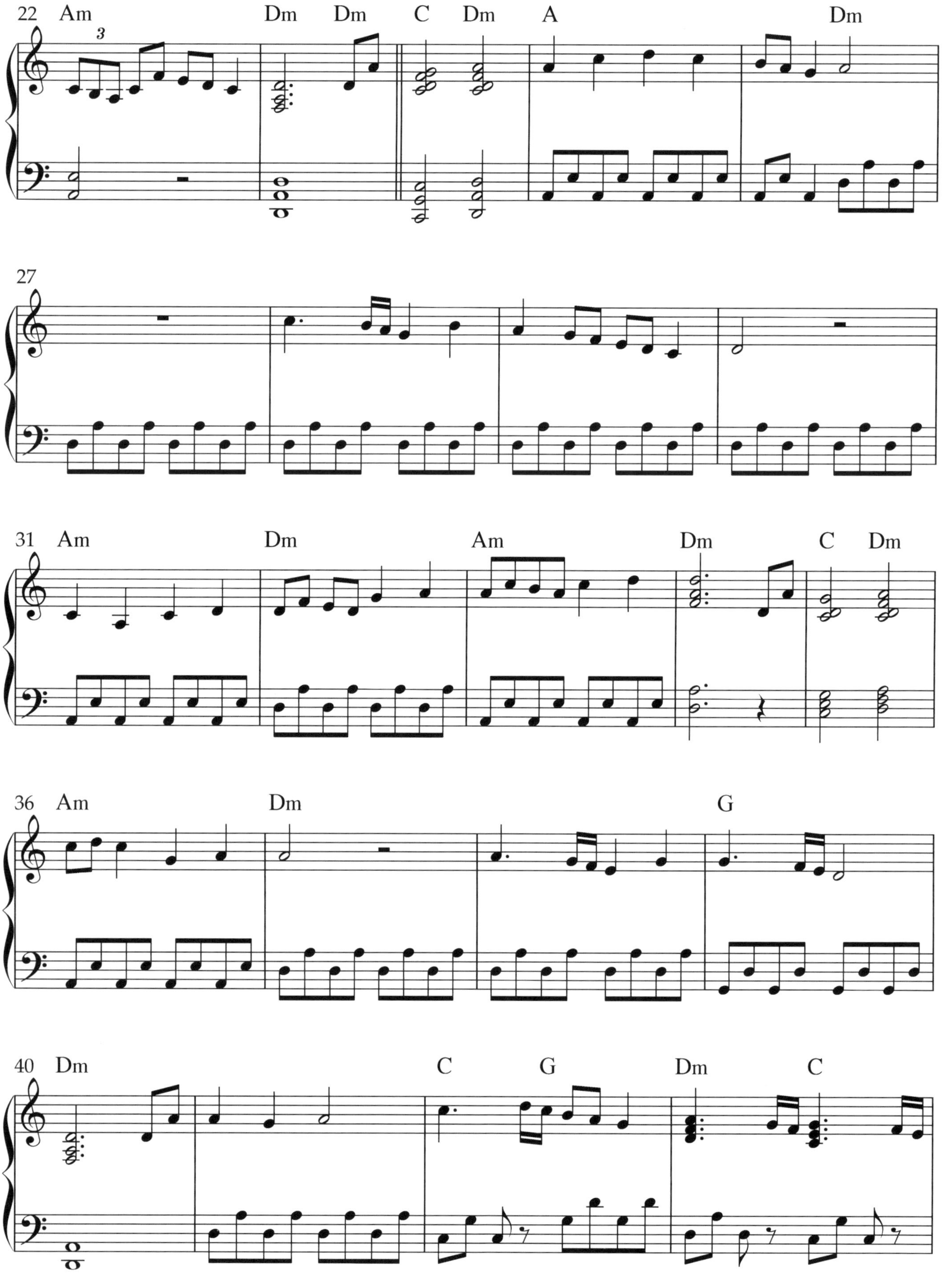
22 Am 3 Dm Dm C Dm A Dm
27
31 Am Dm Am Dm C Dm
36 Am Dm G
40 Dm C G Dm C

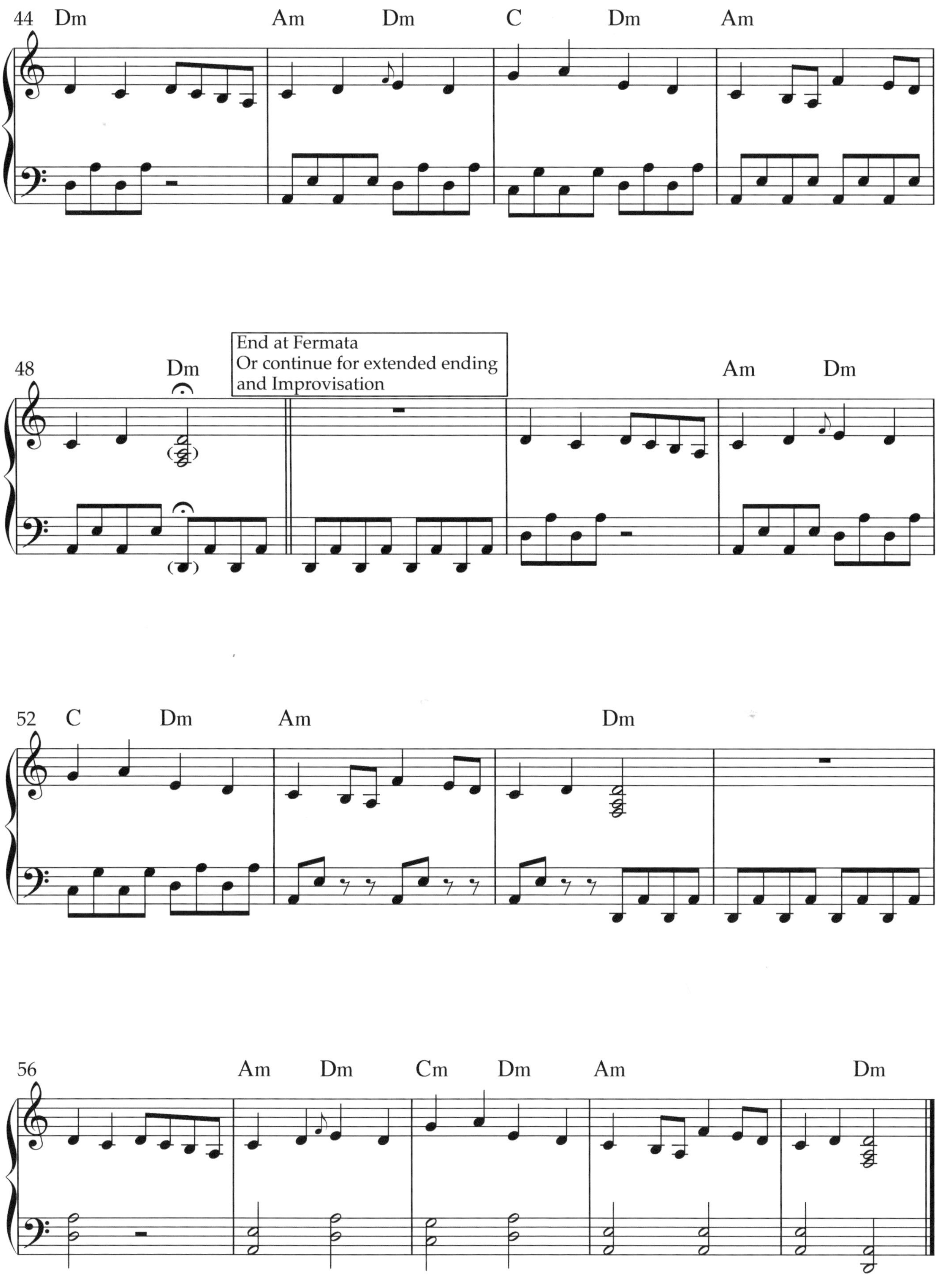
44
Dm
Am
Dm
C
Dm
Am
48
Dm
End at Fermata
Or continue for extended ending
and Improvisation
Am
Dm
52
C
Dm
Am
Dm
56
Am
Dm
Cm
Dm
Am
Dm

De Santa Maria, O Clarissima Mater

17

arr: Monica Schley

Hildegard von Bingen

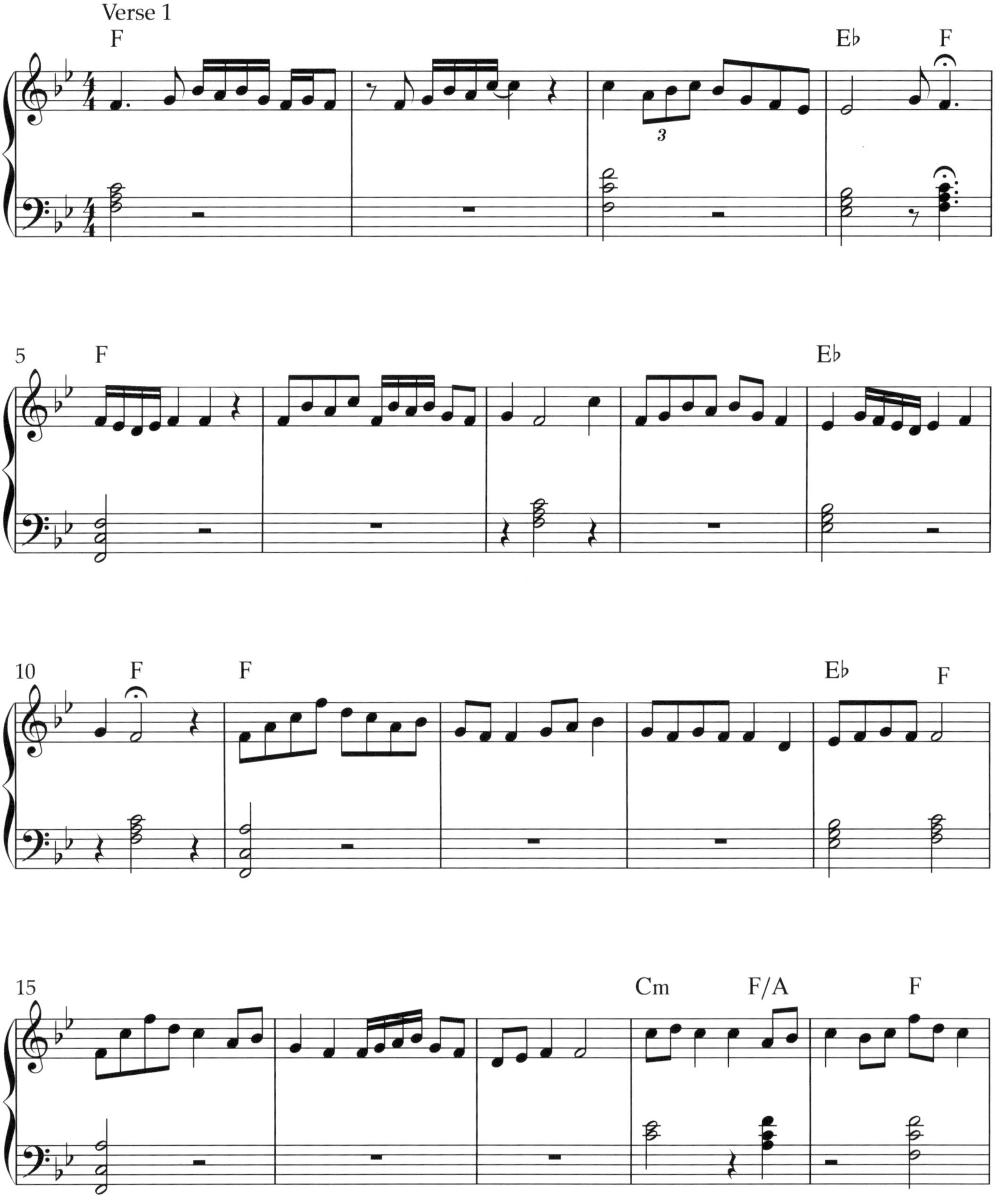

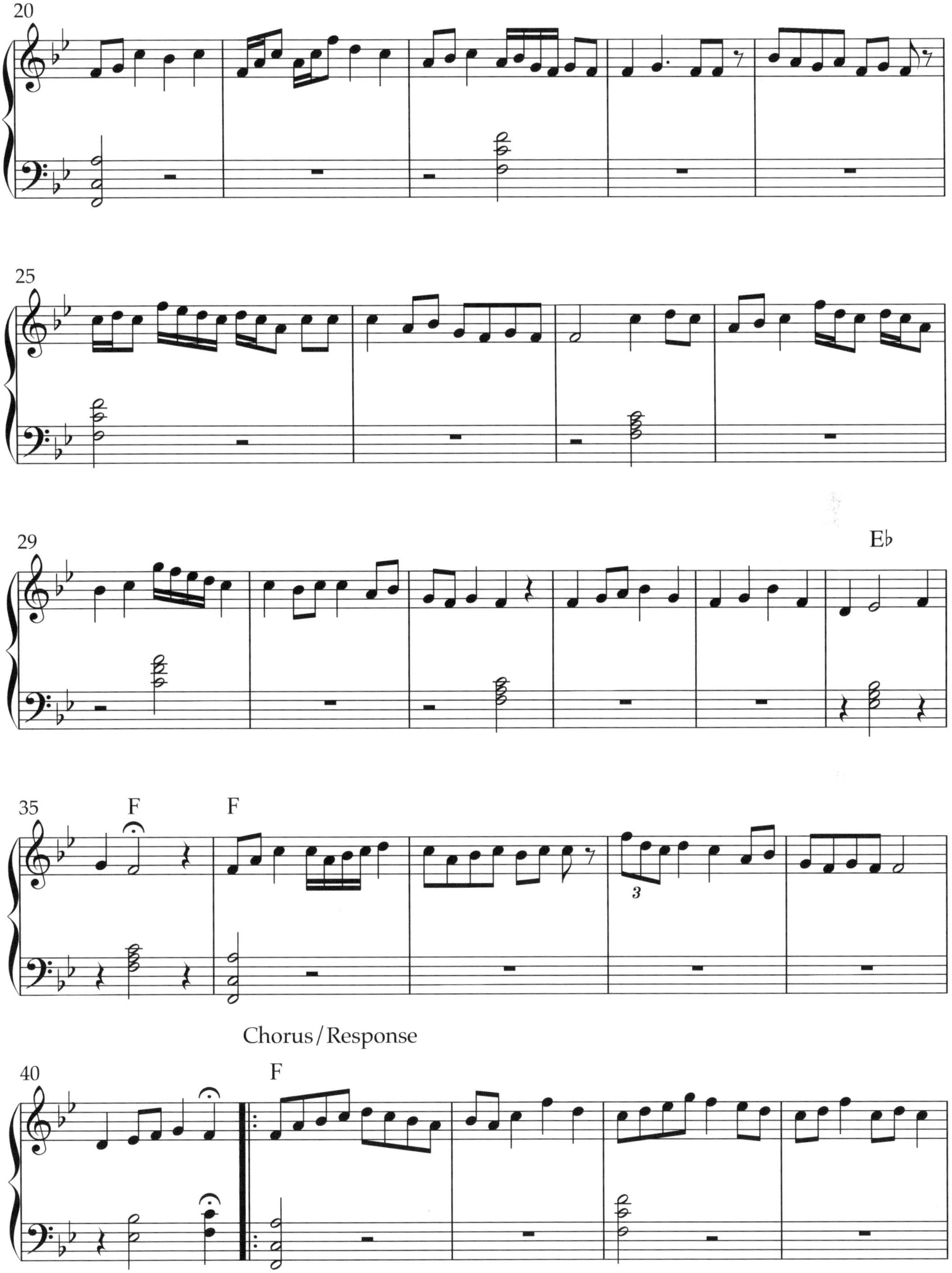
20
25
29
E♭
35
F
F
3
Chorus/Response
40
F

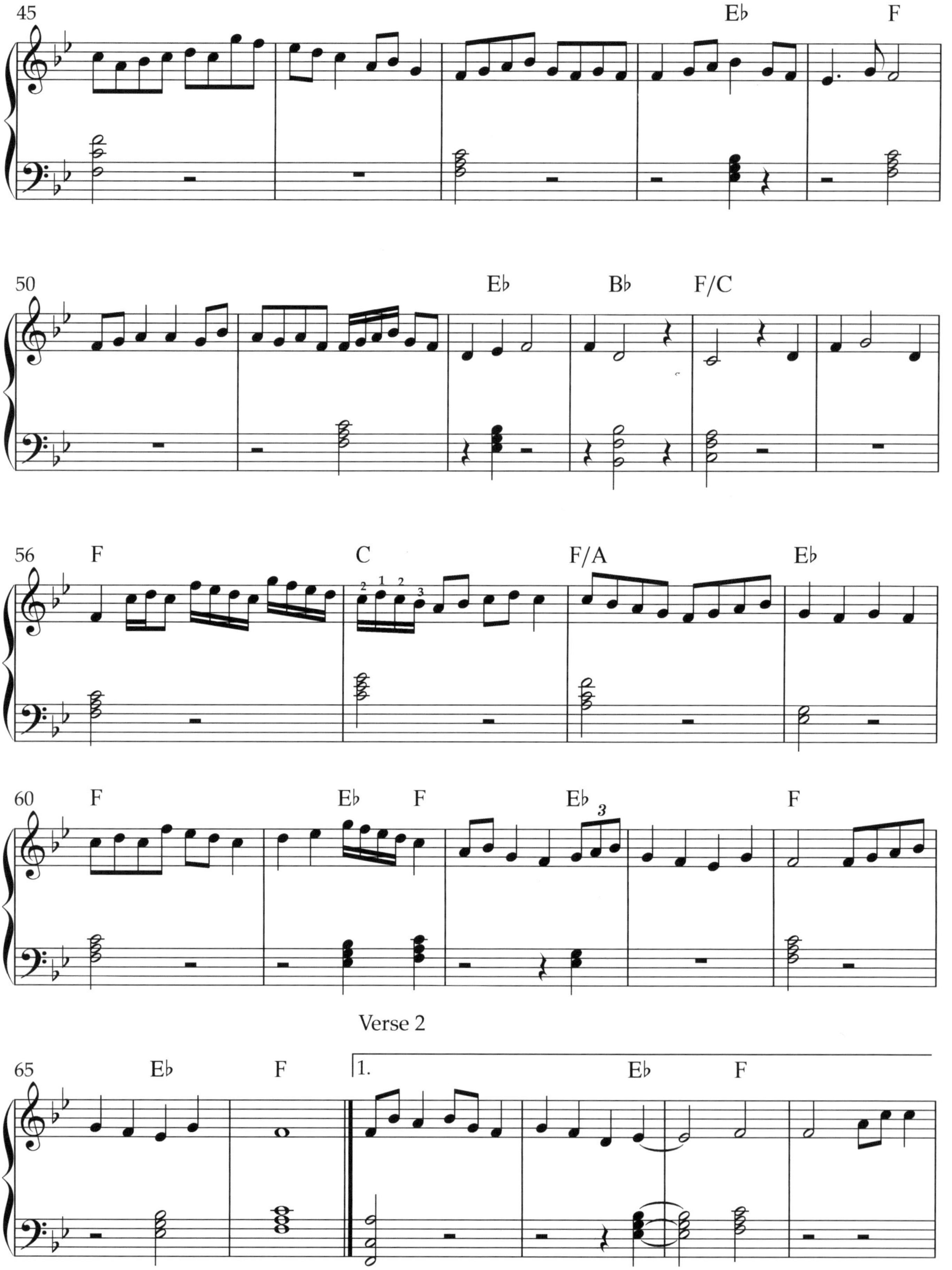
45
E♭
F
50
E♭
B♭
F/C
56
F
C
F/A
E♭
60
F
E♭
F
E♭
F
Verse 2
65
E♭
F
1.
E♭
F

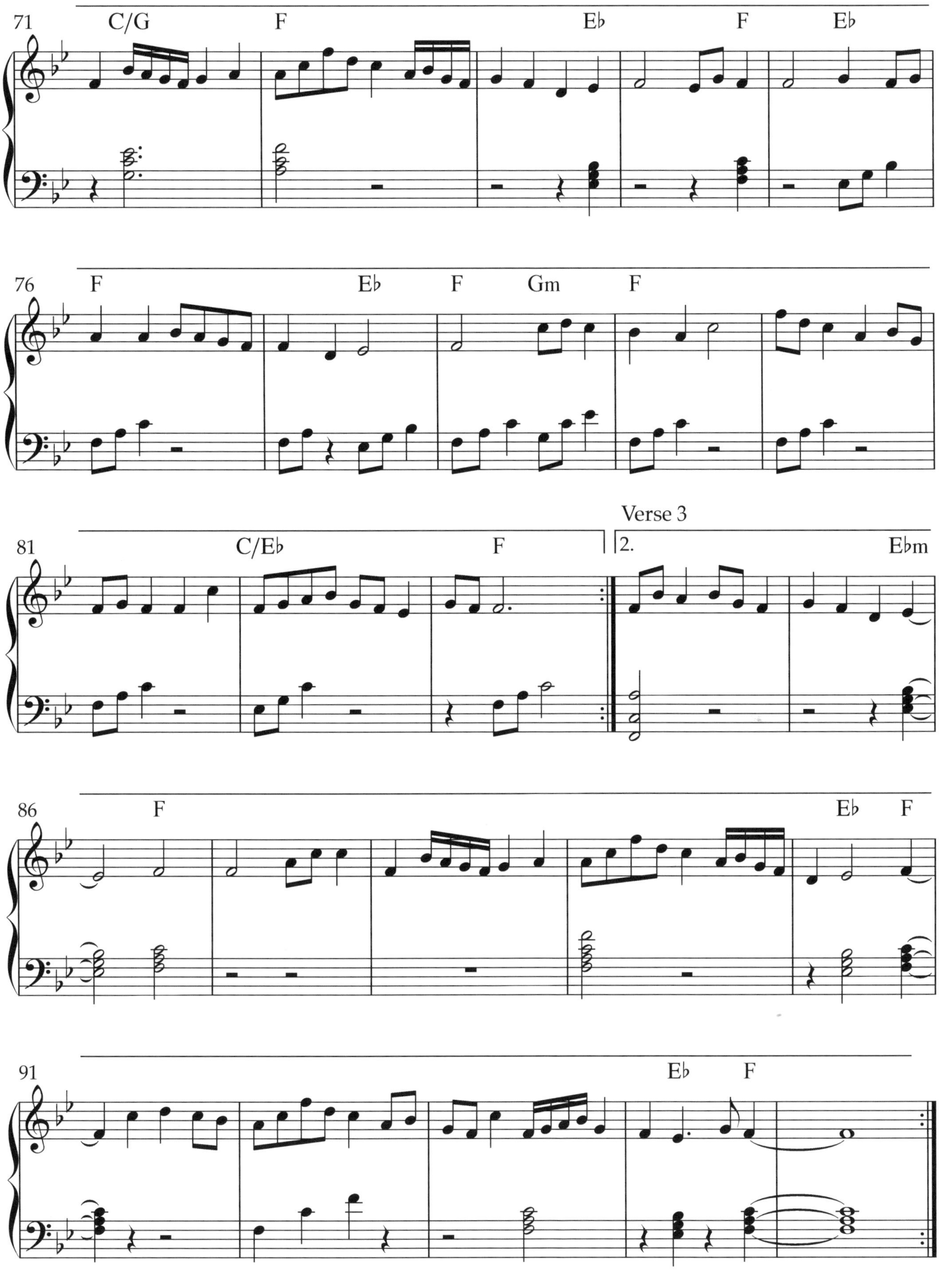
71
C/G
F
E♭
F
E♭
76
F
E♭
F
Gm
F
Verse 3
81
C/E♭
F
2.
E♭m
86
F
E♭
F
91
E♭
F

O Rubor Sanguinis

18

therapy harp arrangement

arr: Monica Schley

Hildegard von Bingen

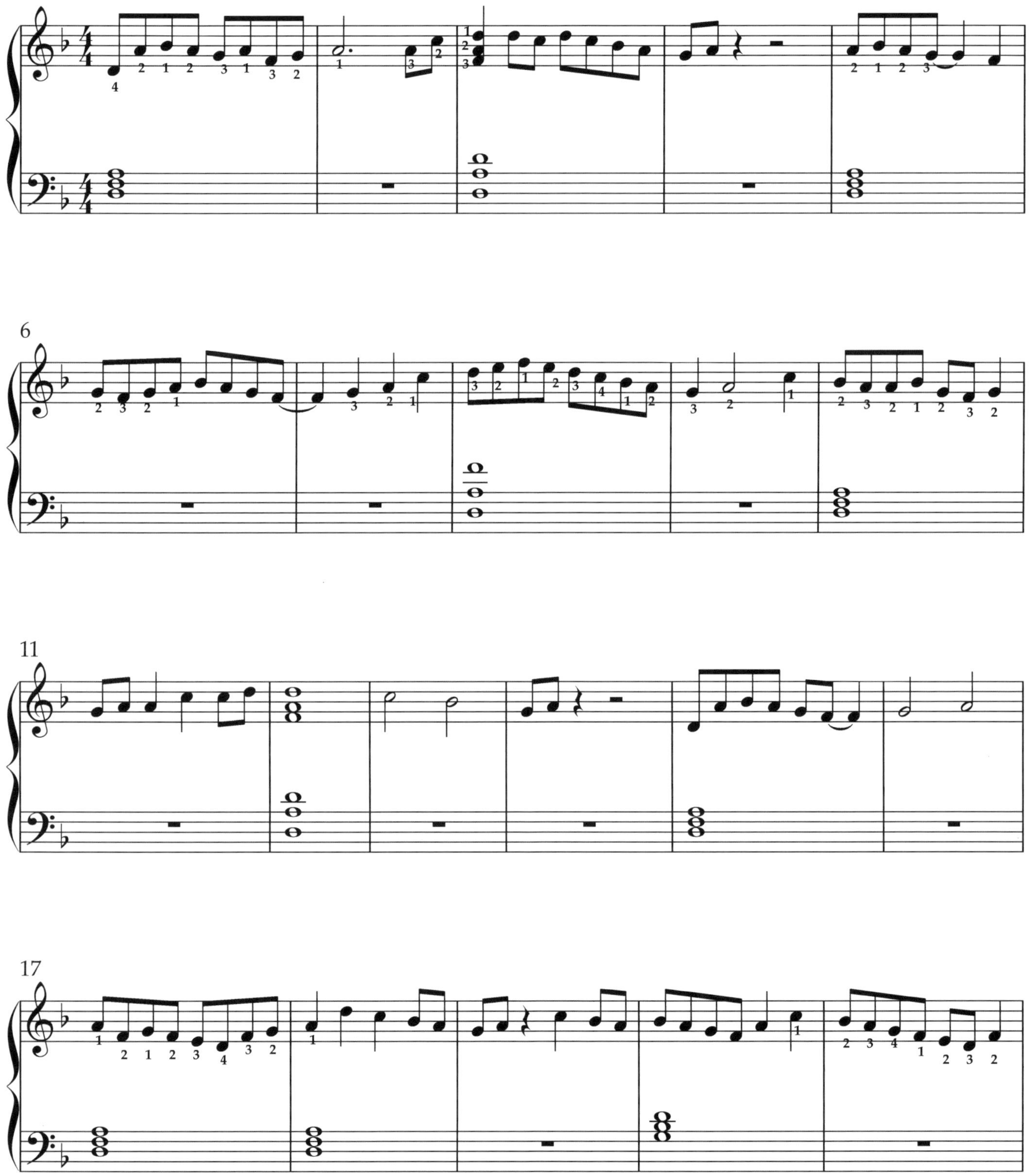

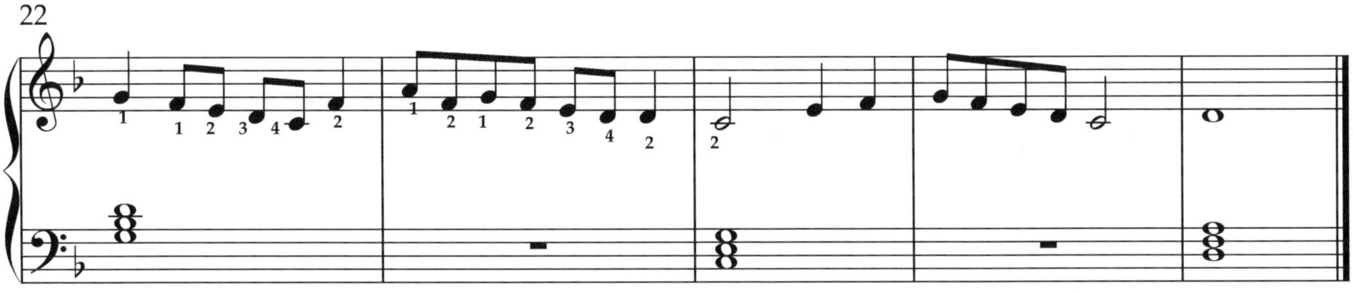
22
1 1 2 3 4 2
1 2 1 2 3 4 2
2

O Rubor Sanguinis

19

arr: Monica Schley

Hildegard von Bingen

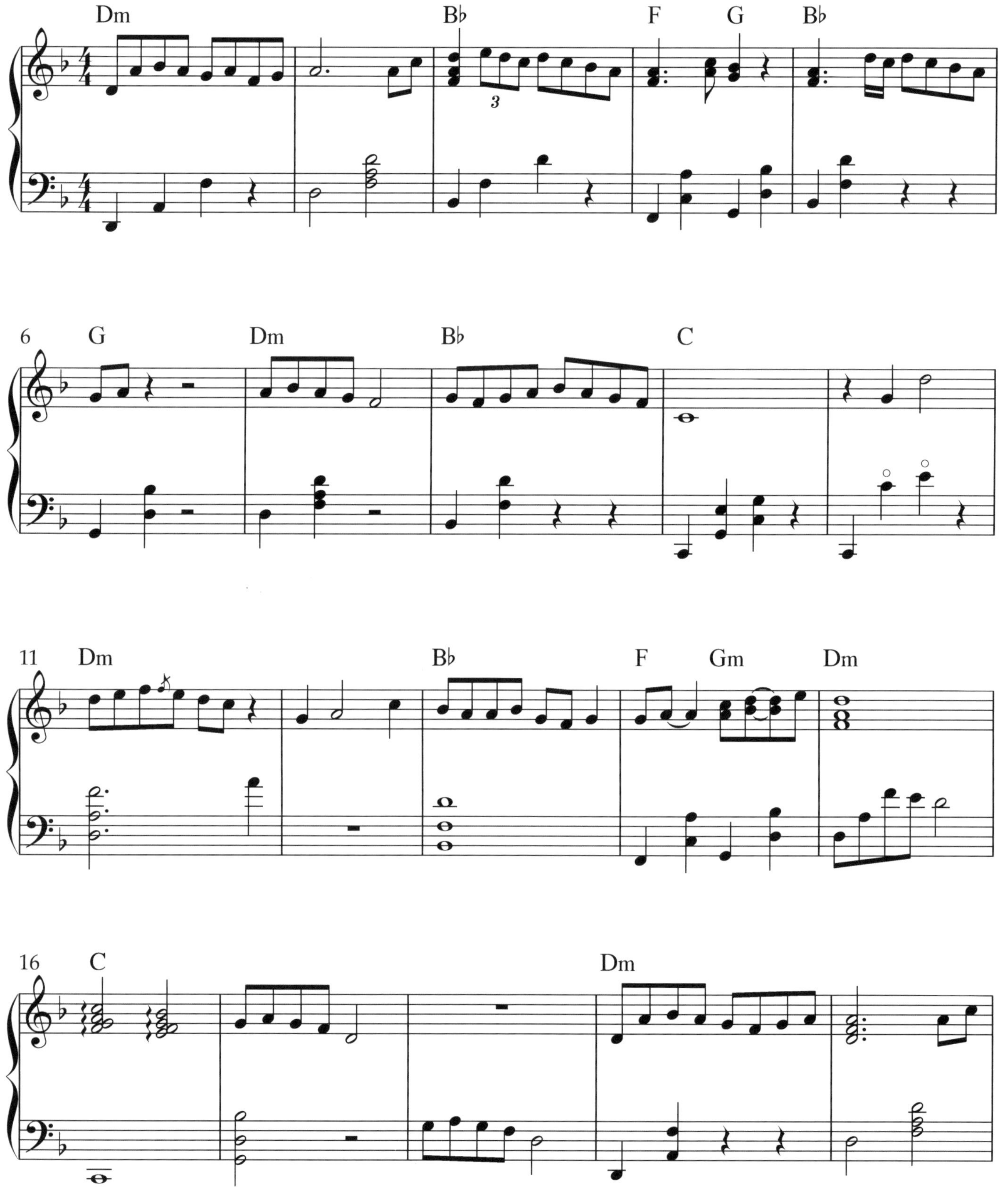

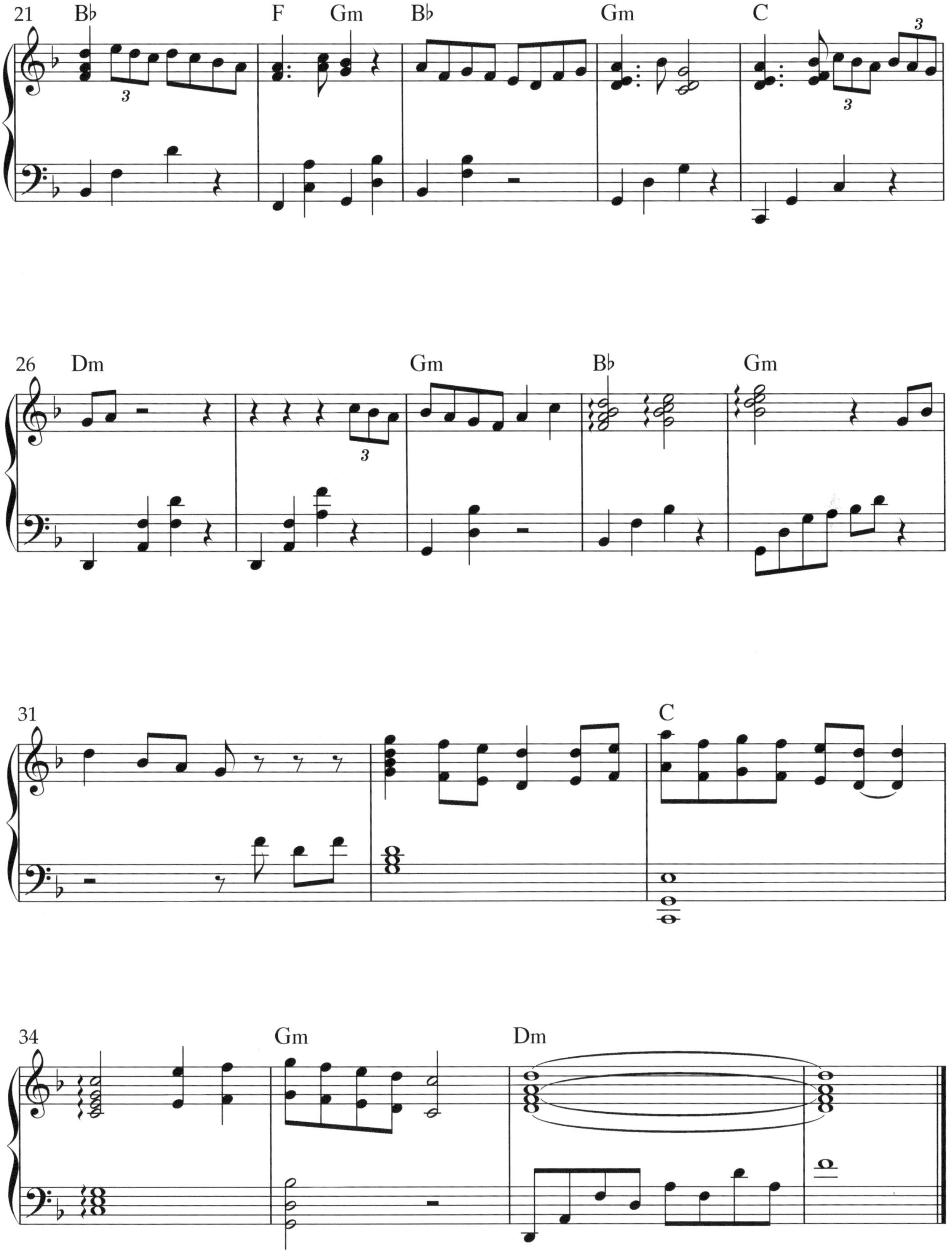
21
B♭
F
Gm
B♭
Gm
C
3
26
Dm
Gm
B♭
Gm
31
C
34
Gm
Dm

Caritas Abundat

Levers: Set 5th Oct B♭

arr: Monica Schley

Hildegard von Bingen

20

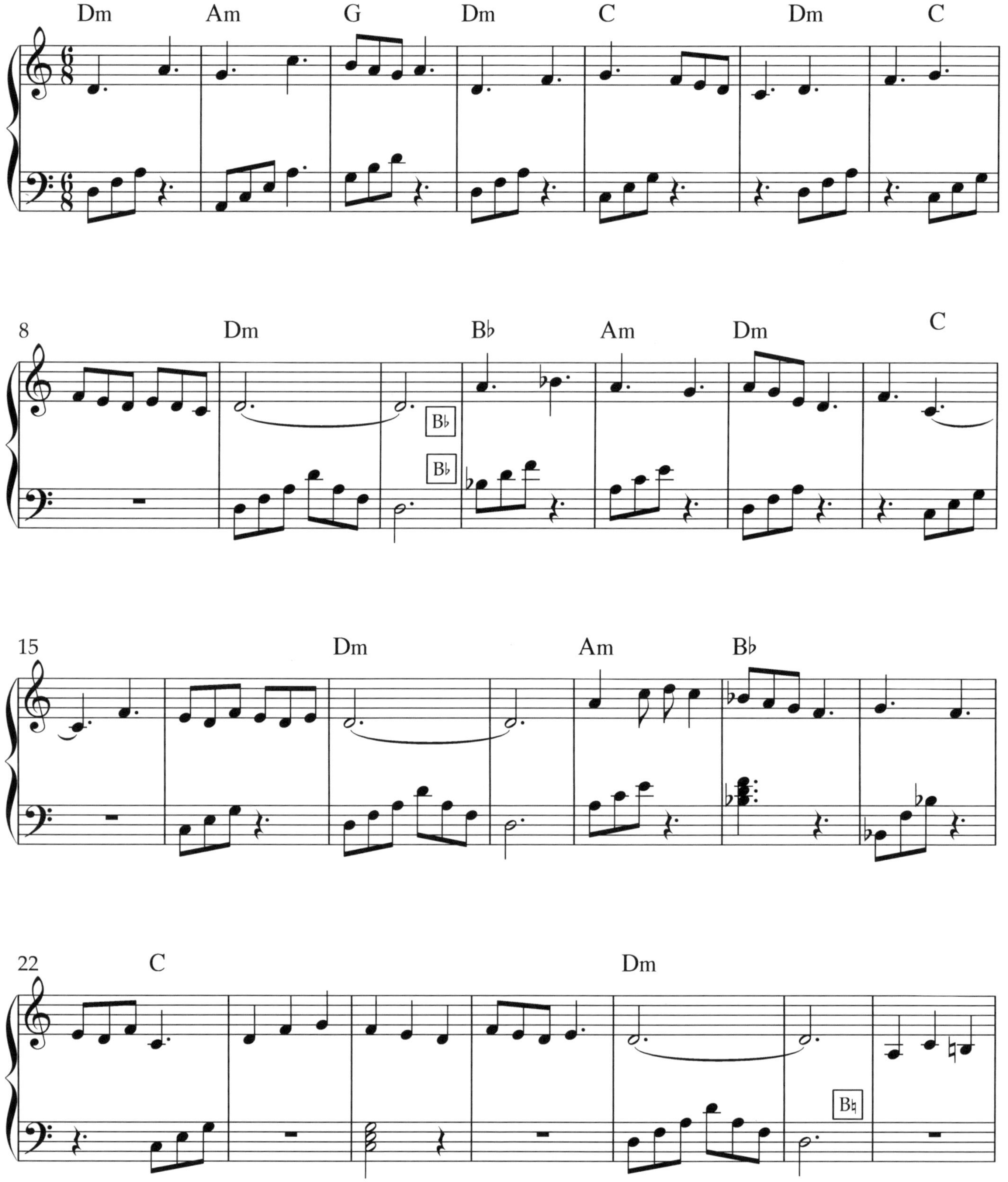

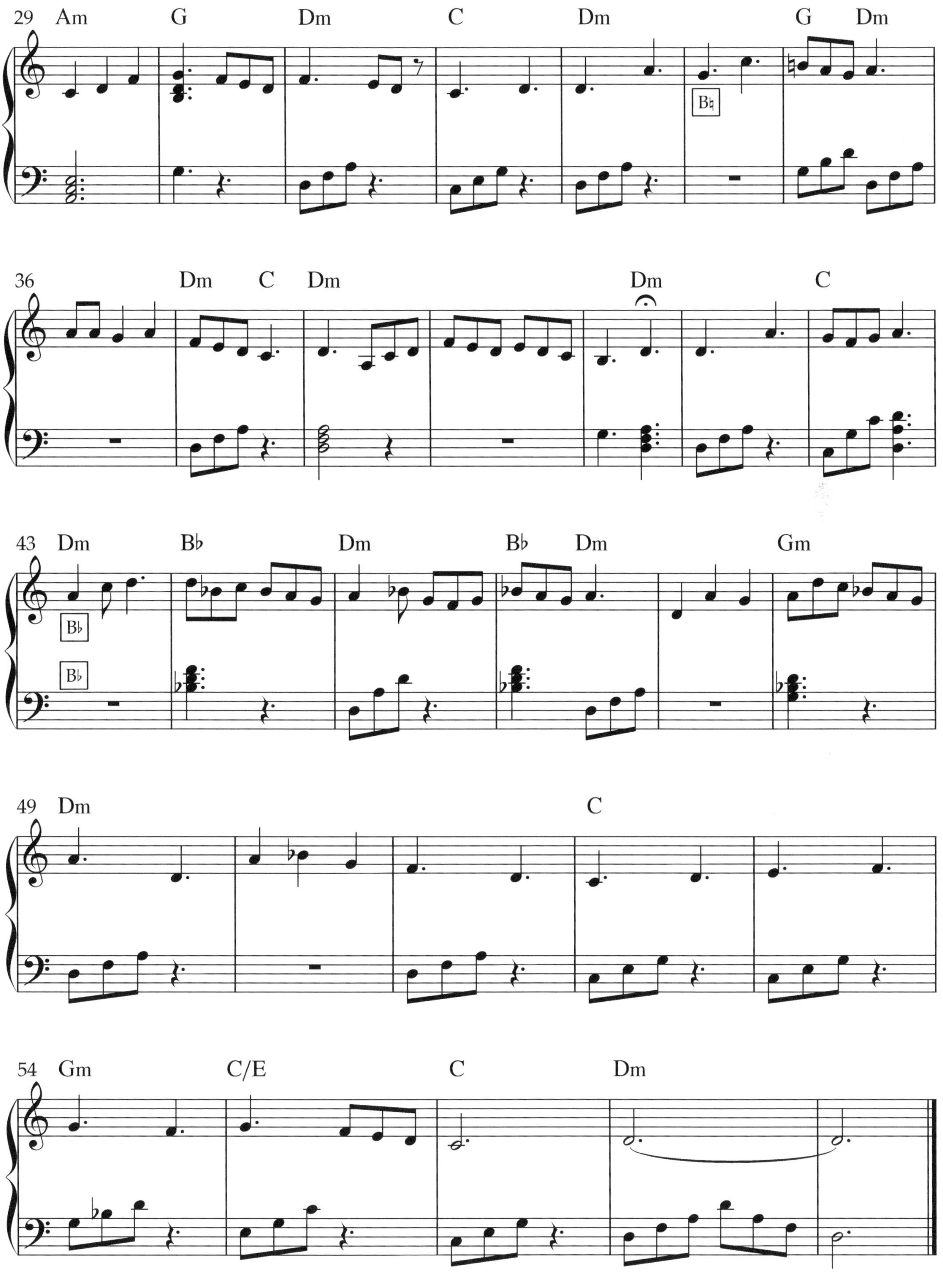
29 Am G Dm C Dm G Dm
B♮
36 Dm C Dm Dm C
43 Dm B♭ Dm B♭ Dm Gm
B♭
B♭
49 Dm C
54 Gm C/E C Dm

About the Arranger

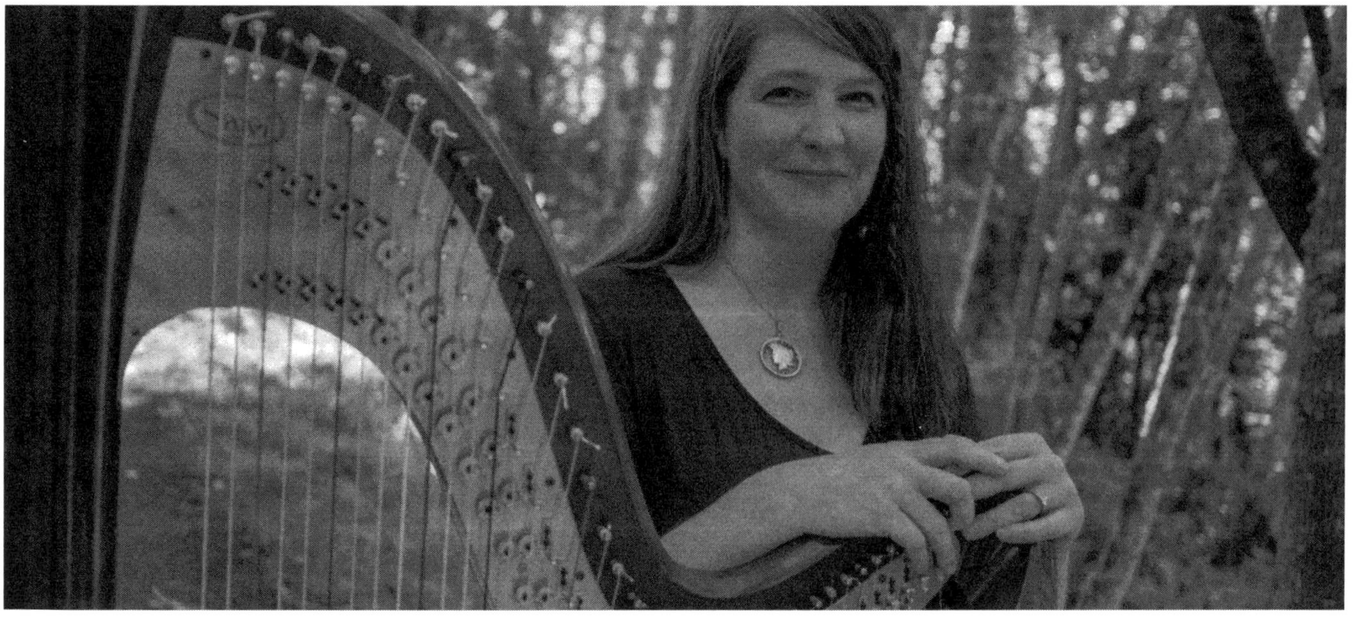

Monica Schley

Monica Schley has been a lifelong musician. She began playing the piano at the age of 4, and by 14, she was studying harp, clarinet, pipe organ, and voice. She first learned about Hildegard von Bingen as a teenager.

In 2015, Monica became a Certified Clinical Musician, playing harp in hospitals and hospice. During that time, she returned to some of Hildegard's music because of its therapeutic sound. However, she realized that arrangements of Hildegard's songs weren't easy to find. So, she arranged a songbook of Hildegard's music for harp.

Monica is an active harp instructor and teaches through her home studio and with Dusty Strings Music School in Seattle, Washington. She has spent over 25 years playing and growing musically in the worlds of classical, jazz, improvisation, Celtic music, and composition. She has gone on to play with a wide array of musicians, including Seattle Rock Orchestra, Jherek Bischoff, Secret Chiefs 3, and Ahamefule Oluo in his critically acclaimed off-Broadway show, "Now I'm Fine." As a composer, Monica led her band, The Daphnes, in their 2015 album, Braids of Kabuya. Monica has received artistic support from the Espy Foundation and Centrum Foundation.

Acknowledgements

First thanks go to Hildegard who continues to inspire the world 1000 years beyond her Earthly living. Thank you to the team at Mel Bay for accepting and publishing this book; to my husband Stephen Schildbach for audio, video, cover art, design and artistic input. Thanks to my students who tested out many arrangements of these songs, especially Neil Hoyt for his fine editorial skills and corrections; to my colleagues who have given me much feedback throughout this book's creation. Thank you also to other musicians and mentors who have paved the way, taught me, and published useful resources: Mona Peck and Melinda Gardiner; Stella Benson; and to my music teachers Francis Miller and Helen Bohman who encouraged me to have academic perseverance, along with musical skills.

Appreciation also goes to Hildegard Publishing, which I discovered through King County Public Library and Seattle Public Library systems. I am grateful to you, dear musician, for purchasing, practicing, and sharing these songs with others.

Thanks to the Source of all Goodness for the gift of music, as it has touched my life in the most extraordinary ways, and for the ability to share this music with others.

May all who listen to and play these songs find peace and well-being.

Other Mel Bay Folk Harp Books

Arranging for Folk Harp (Kim Robertson)

Basic Harp for Beginners (Riley)

Exploring the Folk Harp (Edwards)

First Lessons: Folk Harp (Edwards)

Folk Harp for the Young Beginner (Edwards)

Folk Harp Wall Chart (Edwards)

Fun with the Folk Harp (Goodwin)

Harpsicle Harp Method Book 1 (Walton)

Making Music for Folk Harp (Raimond)

Playing Your Tiny Harp (Riley/Govier)

You Can Teach Yourself Lever Harp (Riley/Kolle)

Celtic Harp Anthology (Edwards)

Celtic Music for Folk Harp (McMichael/Riley)

Christmas Eve (Staneslow)

Christmas Songs for Folk Harp (Bird/Peters)

Classics for Pedal-Free Harp (Bird/Peters)

Dreamtime: Lullabies for Lever and Pedal Harp (S. Williams)

Easy Celtic Harp Solos (Edwards)

Easy Scottish Harp Music (Rondeau)

English Carols for Celtic Harp (Edwards)

WWW.MELBAY.COM

Other Mel Bay Folk Harp Books

Favorite Harp Tunes-Beautiful American Airs and Ballads (Kim Robertson)

Great French Composers for Folk Harp (Staneslow)

Harp Song - The Golden Thread (Umbarger)

Hawaiian Music for Folk Harp (Mitchell)

Hymns & Sacred Songs for Celtic Harp (Edwards)

Irish Harp Music (Doyle)

Kim Robertson: Treasures of the Celtic Harp

Kim Robertson: Celtic Harp Solos

Leith Glass (Thiele)

Light So Brilliant (Claussen)

Medieval & Renaissance Music for Folk Harp (Zaerr)

Medieval Music for Celtic Harp (Edwards)

Mostly Scotch (Bird/Peters)

Music for the Heather Folk (S. Richards)

O'Carolan Tunes for Harp (Fitzgerald)

Scottish Ballads and Aires for Celtic Harp (Kim Robertson)

Tender Shepherd (Kim Robertson)

The Road Home from Skye (Claussen)

Wedding Music for the Lever Harp (Kolle/Riley)

WWW.MELBAY.COM